Charles C. Nelson

Dec '68

TALES
of
TEXAS
and
BEYOND

by
Charles A. Watson

Published by Cedar Elm Publishing Co.
3312 Bellaire Park Court
Fort Worth, Texas 76109

Camellia Debut appeared in ALASKA AIRLINES and THE CAMELLIA JOURNAL under the title *Getting on with Camellias*; a short version of *The Golden Triangle* appeared in THE DALLAS TIMES HERALD.

Library of Congress
Catalog Card Number: 86-71449

ISBN 0-9617161-0-X

For my wife, ELAINE,

Who has made the trip worthwhile

Preface

The personal essay has been on the verge of a comeback ever since Montaigne both invented it and plumbed its depths back in the 1500's. But now--by the end of this century, I'm hoping--this quirky literary form might actually rise again to the stature it deserves. If it happens, it admittedly will be in part by default--due to the throngs of readers fleeing from minimalist fiction and pablum journalism written by underground computers in Pleasantville, New York.

Texans especially like to write personal essays, perhaps because the form allows for exaggeration and even a bald-faced lie every now and then. The Texas literati names of Max Apple, Larry King, Phillip Lopate, and John Graves immediately come to mind--and I know of many others who have quietly pitched their fate with the inventive essay.

The reasons are several, and in part have to do with the times. Readers these days enjoy reading short pieces which at least create the illusion of truth and reality. We like to feel we are learning something, whether it be practical information or philosophical insight. If we can be entertained or amused at the same time, we come away feeling our time has been well-spent--and of course it has.

Writers also are turning to the personal essay because the pieces are so enjoyable to write. Unlike the novelist, a personal essayist doesn't spend ten years laboring on something that might not be any good. Since he most frequently writes about things he already knows, he doesn't kill himself with research, either. Unlike the fiction writer or poet, who so often write out of various vague forms of angst, the personal essayist seems to be a relatively happy person. This pleasant disposition comes through in his writing, leaving his readers feeling that they have made a friend.

Charles Watson enters the writing field with a tremendous advantage; he hasn't spent all his life trying to write. He lived it instead and so now has something to write about. In this one volume he has firmly established a voice all his own, yet one so relatable that the reader can hardly help but identify with his ambitions, remembrances, foibles, and frustrations.

Mainly, though, this writer has the increasingly rare gift of being able to tell a good story. He crosses the artificial boundary between fiction and reality with such seeming ease that you wonder what he does with the rest of the day. The illusion of ease, of course, is part of the magic of the personal essay, and when it comes to magic I wish this one-time accountant and entrepreneur would take a few minutes away from his writing and balance the national budget. He is that good, and I feel privileged to be the one to welcome you to the world according to Charles Watson.

William Allen
Columbus, Ohio
June, 1986

AUTHOR'S NOTE:

William Allen is Director of Creative Writing at Ohio State University and has recently published a winning volume of personal essays entitled, *The Fire in the the Birdbath and Other Disturbances.* Bill is also my friend. Without exaggeration, the following pieces would still lie inert and disconnected in the cave of my unconscious had it not been for the spark of his teaching.--CAW

CONTENTS

Prologue: Frank Dobie, Move Over

The year was 1939. As the train rolled across the countryside north of Houston, I took out my new pencil to write a letter home and let my folks know I was already riding first class in a Pullman. I got as far as "Dear Folks" when the train began whizzing past another small station. I caught a glimpse of car headlights waiting at a crossing, and I heard the short, quick clanging of a bell. Then we were out in the countryside again.

Writing was easy on a train as smooth as this. I was using the black lead end of my new pencil, which also had a red lead end like all professional accountants' pencils. Besides the pencil, Miss Parker had given me a new leather briefcase and a diary to log my time charges and expenses. Mr. Beasley had said I'd be living in hotels and charging all my expenses to clients, leaving my salary free and clear. The diary and all the audit working papers I would need were in my new briefcase on the seat beside my new hat.

I'd have to tell in my letter about the new hat, I decided. Mr. Beasley had gone with me to deposit my first paycheck in a client bank, and on the way back he had suggested I buy a hat. We stopped in

Battelstein's (also a client) and found one that looked like Mr. Beasley's, but lighter in color. (His was a shade of gray that looked old when it was new.)

The Pullman was so quiet that I could hear snatches of conversation now and then. I could also hear the fellow across the aisle smacking the apple he had just begun to eat. Except for the apple and his wooden leg, which was propped on the seat, he reminded me of Professor J. Frank Dobie at the University in Austin. In my sophomore year, I'd had to drop out of Professor Dobie's writing class because of a conflict with an accounting course I'd really needed. But I was in the class long enough to find out what Professor Dobie thought about writing. He said writers had to be so dedicated that they would be willing to go hungry. That had made dropping the class easier, for at the time I was dedicated to making money--as much and as fast as I could.

We were on a curve now, and I was watching the long string of lights in the cars, when the porter came in announcing the first call for dinner. Almost everyone got up and began filing out--everyone except me and the man with the wooden leg. The porter stopped between us and leaned over me to pick up my new hat off the seat.

"Let me get this out of your way, suh," he said. After picking it up, he spread his fingers inside the crown to avoid touching the felt. "I won't have to brush this hat, no suh!" He hung it on a high brass hook I hadn't noticed. "Will you be having dinner with us tonight, suh?"

I told him I would as soon as I finished my letter. After he turned away, I looked out the window wondering how I could express to my folks the way I felt about my train ride. This was what I had always wanted. This was what I called really living.

After the porter left the car, the man across the aisle set his wooden leg on the floor and began digging in a hand valise. Soon he brought out two more apples and held them across the aisle to me.

"You're welcome to one of these," he said.

"Oh, no, thanks. I'll be going to the diner in a few minutes."

It was then I noticed the hat hanging on another brass hook above his head; it was a ranch-style hat, like the one Professor Dobie wore.

The fellow smacked for a while, then paused. "I haven't learned to walk very well on solid ground yet, let alone on a moving train. I'm staying down as much as I can."

"Did you just lose your leg?" I wouldn't ordinarily ask a person about his wooden leg, but the fellow seemed to want to talk about it.

"Almost a year ago at my sawmill. My home-town doctor drove me to Houston, hoping the specialists there could save it. But they couldn't. I've just been down there to get fitted with this new contraption."

Without standing, he took his pants down to show me the cushion and all the leather straps. There wasn't anyone in the car except us, but he hadn't even looked. He kept on talking while he pulled his pants back up.

"Before they took my leg off, I made the doctors promise to save it for me. They did. It's been in the freezer all this time. That leg was a part of me. Now I'm taking it home to bury it. It's in the baggage car with my crutches."

The train began slowing down, and my new

acquaintance closed his valise and reached for his hat. When the train came to a complete stop at the station, I got up and offered him my arm. He shook his head.

"The sooner I learn to walk on this thing without my crutches, the better."

I followed him down the aisle and watched as the porter helped him off the train. After tipping the porter, he looked up at me and said, "Too bad you're just passing through. I'd invite you to the funeral."

As the train pulled out of the station, I thought about how in my chosen profession, my new employers wanted me to be impersonal and skeptical. And this was what I was trying to become. Yet that frozen leg yarn somehow put me on the spot. If I had decided to become a writer instead of an accountant, a tale like this would have been a good one to write about in a letter to my folks. But that would have taken a lot of time, and I was in a hurry.

I am not in as big a hurry now as I was then. I have the time to write letters and much more, but it isn't all that easy. Maybe Professor Dobie was right. Maybe you can't be a writer unless you starve first. Pullman windows are scarce now, but I'll bet I spend as much time looking out of other windows as Steinbeck or O'Connor ever did.

I'm beginning to believe that becoming a writer probably takes a lifetime. When the train stopped that day to let my one-legged acquaintance off, perhaps I should have laid aside my accountant's pencil, handed my new hat to the porter, and got off with him.

The Lively Undertaking Business

My experience in the undertaking business started in the casket room, where I spent Saturday afternoons prying open shipping boxes, hauling away excelsior, and being a messenger for my dad and Mr. Eubanks who operated the business along with a general store.

Around four o'clock in the afternoon, I often found the satin softness of the caskets irresistible. I would take off my shoes and slip into one for a nap, knowing that everyone else was busy in the adjoining store.

One Saturday afternoon I was asleep in a casket with the lid propped open when Mr. Eubanks came in with a delegation to make a selection. Mr. Eubanks awakened me in a voice loud enough to raise the dead. I snapped up like a jack-in-the-box, and when I began twisting out, a stampede broke loose as the entire delegation tried to get through the door at the same time. Mr. Eubanks broke up laughing. Afterwards, he told the story of the stampede so many times that now I suspect it was his way of warning me.

By the time I reached sixteen, I was a veteran in all phases of the operation except embalming.

Besides working in the casket room, I had driven the hearse, handled the flowers, and ushered at the funerals. It was about this time my dad gave me the added job of driving the store's model A delivery truck and hired a black boy my age named Punkin as my co-worker.

When Punkin and I weren't on a delivery or in the casket room, we worked in the rear of the general store itself. We blended coffee, candled eggs, tested butter fat, filled cooking oil and vinegar jugs, and carried out flour, corn meal, and heavy packages to the wagons outside.

The rear of the store was a crowded place. Flour bins, hardware shelves, and crates of eggs lined the walls, and leather harnesses hung from the ceiling. Casks of cooking oil and vinegar, and bags of coffee and chicory, gave off an odorous tang which ripened to full strength when black men congregated around the red-hot wood stove in winter smoking their pipes and nickel cigars, dipping snuff, or chewing Brown Mule. Within the veil of tobacco smoke, they punctuated their loud talk with shots into the sand box beneath the stove and lowered their voices only for Mr. Eubanks who came by at least once every Saturday afternoon to shake hands and to call each man by name.

Not everyone was as gracious as Mr. Eubanks, whether they were dealing with whites, blacks, or boys like me and Punkin. One of the most unfriendly of all was Mr. Hiram Perkins, an eccentric farmer but a good customer. While lacking in kindness and a sense of humor, Mr. Hiram was not a bad man, just cantankerous-- brought on, some said, by living alone and doing his own cooking. They said his cooking would curdle a hog's stomach and had made him do such things as wear out a buggy whip on a cultivator. I'd never heard of his injuring anyone seriously, but Punkin and I thought he had that in mind one Saturday afternoon when we made a delivery to his farm. He was waiting with a buggy whip behind his back when we pulled up to his barn with a load of cow feed.

As soon as we got out of the truck, he snapped his whip and hollered, "Which one of you whelps poured vinegar in my cooking oil jug?" When we just stood there, he popped it again. "Which one?" he yelled.

I saw Punkin's jaw working, but no sounds were coming out. When Mr. Hiram started around the truck after him, Punkin bolted, making a beeline for the house. Mr. Hiram took off too, popping his whip at Punkin's heels. When they disappeared behind the house, I feared for Punkin's life, but in no time they emerged on the other side with my black friend two whip lengths in the lead.

As they were circling a second time, I came to my senses and cranked up the truck. Soon Punkin reappeared and, seeing the truck underway, came racing toward me at top speed. When he jumped on the running board, I gave the truck plenty of gas. Looking back, I saw Mr. Hiram beating the ground with his whip.

It was almost closing time when Punkin and I got back to the store. After we told what happened, Mr. Eubanks and my dad shook their heads. Then they told us to be more careful.

That very evening, Mr. Eubanks roused my dad with the news that Mr. Hiram had died. He asked Dad to please go out there and pick up the body. He also suggested to Dad that he take me along for the experience.

I was feeling so guilty I didn't know whether I was afraid to go or not. I had never seen a dead person outside of a casket before and certainly had no desire to see Mr. Hiram again, dead or alive. I was caught between a wish to be with my dad and a fear of finding out for sure what I thought was the cause of Mr. Hiram's sudden death.

When we stopped at the store for a stretcher, the town night watchman came over to see what was going on.

"Who died?" he asked.

"Hiram Perkins," Dad said, slamming the rear door of the ambulance.

The night watchman stood aside. "Is Hiram Perkins dead?"

Dad muttered, "He better be."

I didn't blame Dad. It was the same pointless question people always asked when told so-and-so had died--just as if you had been kidding the first time you told them.

We left the night watchman standing in the middle of the street and headed out of town, following a red gravel road until we reached the Perkins farm. When we stopped in front of the house, I could see someone sitting on the porch, silhouetted by the hallway lamp light. Out of the stillness, a man's voice greeted us.

"You made good time."

"That you Dolph?" My dad spoke quietly.

"Hiram's laid out in the parlor," Dolph said, motioning to the front room on the right.

The light breeze through the open hallway brought an odor of cooking oil from the kitchen. Most houses in the country smelled like cooking oil, even after they were abandoned.

Dad picked up the hallway lamp. "I think I'll go in."

"Sure," Dolph said, getting up and following him into the parlor.

I lagged behind, peering from the doorway. Mr. Hiram lay rigid on the bed, in the same clothes he had worn when he chased Punkin. "Where'd you find him?" Dad whispered.

Dolph led Dad to the hallway and pointed to a shot-gun lying in the shadows. "Right there by the gun." Then he walked to the wall. "Look at this hole where the telephone used to be. I think Hiram felt a spell coming on and tried to get central and couldn't. Maybe somebody was on the party line and wouldn't get off. Hiram wasn't too popular, you know. He must have got madder and madder. Maybe he got so mad he blew the consarned phone off the wall."

Suddenly, a groan floated out of the parlor.

Dad whirled and ran. Dolph followed, quickly. I went in too, but slowly. Mr. Hiram was thrashing around as if Mr. Eubanks had hollered at him the way he hollered at me that day in the casket room. Dad grabbed his arms and Dolph got hold of a leg. I was petrified until Dad yelled, "Don't just stand there! Grab the other leg!"

Mr. Hiram fought like a wild man. His chest heaved up and down and his face twisted and turned red. I was doubting how much longer I could hold on when he relaxed. After a while, his breathing settled down, and he opened his eyes. Looking up at Dad, he said, "Is that you, Edd? What're you doing in my house?"

Although Mr. Hiram seemed fully recovered from

his spell, I dreaded going out there on deliveries. And I was horrified by the thought of someday having to go for bodies in the middle of the night, alone, and not knowing whether the night watchman's question, "Is so-and-so dead?", was pointless or not.

By the time I graduated from high school, I'd already begun making other plans. After the graduation ceremony, Mr. Eubanks surprised me with a crisp fifty-dollar bill. "I hear you're going to Tyler Commercial College," he said, beaming at me as I stood in my graduation cap and gown. "When you finish, I'm counting on you to come back and help us in the undertaking department. Don't let that College talk you into doing anything different, son. You'd make us a cracker-jack."

The Golden Triangle

◞◠◟◞◠◟

While we waited for Sam, we watched the glow in the sky from the East Texas oil field.

"You want to be careful when you get down to where that glow is coming from," Dad said. "'The Golden Triangle' is a wild place."

The Golden Triangle was what they had commenced calling Gladewater, Kilgore, and Longview, the three towns that made a triangle where the oil field was. I wouldn't be there long. As soon as I saved enough, I was going to Tyler Commercial College.

Sam had a night clerk's job in The Golden Triangle. When he arrived, Dad asked him where he stayed.

"At Miss Belle's rooming house. She also owns the hotel where I work. She's spudding in a well across the street from the rooming house."

Just then Mother came out with the box of cookies, which for me was a combination offering and blessing that took some of the sting out of leaving.

On the way to The Golden Triangle, Sam and I ate all the cookies, then at midnight, as we drove up to the rooming house, I could see as well as hear the drilling rig across the street. It was pounding away, and you could read the newspaper by the light from the boiler. After we went to bed, I lay awake watching the shadows on the wall until the rhythm of the pounding finally put me to sleep.

Our rooming house was about three blocks from the middle of town. Swarms of people crowded the sidewalks and sometimes overflowed into the streets which were jammed with wagons, trucks, and cars. A morning shower had muddied everything. But the soldiers I saw were spic and span except for the mud on their boot soles.

I had read that some people were mad at the Governor for sending soldiers to The Golden Triangle. Some allowed their wells to flow against his orders, controlling the oil from valves hidden in secret places. Some even took pot shots at the soldiers.

And that was why the Texas Ranger, Lone Wolf Gonzaullus, was here. Lone Wolf took calisthenics every morning and kept the hammers of his guns half-cocked. He said he'd rather be tried for killing six outlaws than have one tried for killing him. I never said anything to Sam, but I really did want Lone Wolf's autograph.

Just before my money ran out, I got a daytime job stacking shelves and helping the butcher in a grocery next door to the hotel where Sam worked. One drizzly November day, a large red-headed lady in a fur coat came limping up to the butcher's display case where I was cleaning out moldy meat. She leaned her cane against the case, threw open her fur coat, and rested her over-sized chest on the counter-top which was warm from the lights inside. I recognized her from Sam's description, although

I'd never seen her before.

"You must be Sam's friend," Miss Belle said, tapping a cigarette on the counter. I'd never seen anyone with as much powder and paint on her face except at the circus. She took a deep draw from her cigarette and blew smoke across the counter. "Where's the butcher, drunk again?"

While I was telling her the butcher was in the cooler, she began to cough. She coughed so hard her face showed red through all that white powder. In a little while she raised her arms, gasping for air.

"I'm fine, honey," she said. "Go tell the butcher to put his pint away and come out here. I want to buy some fresh turkeys."

When I came back, Miss Belle said, "I got something else on my mind. Why don't you come next door for a little chit-chat after I get through here?"

I was nodding that I would just as the butcher dumped an arm load of dressed turkeys on the meat block. Miss Belle said she wanted some nice ones for her kids at the the orphan's home. That was where Sam and I had delivered some broken-down rooming house furniture a week ago.

When I walked in the hotel a few minutes later, I could see that most of the lobby furniture needed carting off as well. The dead cigar smell in the place reminded me of what Sam said about the cuspidors: cleaning them was almost as bad as looking after Miss Belle's husband, Sylvester. Then I saw Miss Belle motioning to me.

As I walked up, she said, "Come in, Sonny." She had to grip her knee with both hands to swivel around because of an odd-shaped shoe on her left foot.

She said, "I want you to work nights when Sam goes on days. I can use a boy that can handle Sylvester and keep his mouth shut." Pointing to a pile of mail, she continued, "I'm on a committee that's covered me up with letter-writing, and I understand you know how to type."

"Yes, Ma'am, a little. I'm just learning."

"That's good enough. I'll pay you what you're making and you ought to get some tips."

About a week after I started on my new job, Sylvester came in one night later and drunker than usual. He leaned on my desk, breathing whiskey in my face.

"Ever time I come in, you're sittin' at that typewriter. You can't have no fun that way. Come with me, sonny-boy, and we'll go to Mattie's Ball Room and dance, dance, dance!"

He swung across the lobby, twirling as if he were dancing. His feet tangled with a cuspidor; he lost his balance and went sprawling on the floor. When I got him to his feet, he pushed me away, pulled a pint out of his coat pocket, and drained it. After running his tongue around the mouth of the empty bottle, he tried to put it on the corner of my desk, but it slipped from his fingers and broke when it hit the floor.

With great care, he kicked the broken glass under my desk then began to slap his pockets, swaying so much I grabbed his arm.

"Leave me alone, dammit," he said, jerking his arm away. "I'm tryin' afine my money. I need a nightcap."

Finally, he pulled a fistfull of bills from his pocket and stuck them in my face.

"Here, Sonny. Go get me a pint."

"It's three in the morning, Sylvester," I said.

"Everything's closed."

"Damn", he said, sitting down abruptly in my chair. His chin dropped, and his face looked so mournful I thought he was going to cry. But he didn't protest when I got him to his feet and began marching him down the hall.

As we were passing Miss Belle's door, he balked, saying if I was his friend, I'd slip in there and get him a pint. But I kept going and got him into his room and onto his bed. When I hung up his pants, a wad of bills fell out. I put the money under his pillow, and I locked the door on my way out as Miss Belle had ordered.

For an hour, it was very peaceful. Then out of the blue the phone rang. It was Sam. "Where's Miss Belle?" he hollered, so loud he hurt my ear.

"In her room," I said. "Why? What's going on?" He said all hell had broken loose, and to tell Miss Belle to hide, she'd know where, and that he had to hang up and would come back when it was safe.

I ran down to Miss Belle's door, opened it with my master key, and bumped a table as I felt my way across the unfamiliar sitting room. I heard her yell, "Stop! I'll shoot anybody that touches that door."

I stopped dead. But when I told her about Sam's call, she coughed and said, "Come in."

She was bent over working with her odd-shaped shoe. Her cane, gun, and a bottle of whiskey lay on a table beside a wheel attached to a rod that went through the wall. I had seen clusters of wheels like this on completed oil wells which gaugers called "Christmas trees." The gaugers turned the wheels to open and close valves that controlled the oil flow.

After helping her to stand, I told her about Sylvester. She uncapped the pint, took a swig, and murmured, "I guess I'm gonna have to shoot him."

We crossed the hall and found Sylvester asleep. After gathering up all the bills I could find, I passed them to Miss Belle. Then we walked down the hall to a narrow door marked "Service" which I had thought was a cleaning closet.

Miss Belle unlocked the door with a key she took from her wrist. A small room, just big enough for a cot, a chair, a lavatory, and a toilet lay before us. By compressing herself, Miss Belle squeezed sidewise through the door.

"When the soldiers come," she said, "tell them I've gone and you don't know where." She closed the door, and I heard the lock click as I turned away.

I was glad when the soldiers finally came. They flanged out in front of the hotel, taking orders from a trim, neat man in a white Stetson who marched quickly into the lobby with a hand on one of his guns and the other hand grasping a pair of handcuffs. He looked all around then asked me, "Where's Anna Belle Sylvester? I got a warrant for her." I was sure Miss Belle could hear him in her hiding place.

"I don't know, sir."

"Where's her room?"

"The first one on the left, sir. But she's gone, sir." (I wished I could have said "Lone Wolf" instead of "sir").

"Give me the key."

I did. And Lone Wolf said, "You stay right here."

After knocking on Miss Belle's door with the butt of his pistol, he turned the lock, kicked the door open, then crouched, sweeping his gun across the opening. In about ten seconds, he went in and closed the door.

When Lone Wolf came out, his guns were in their

holsters, but he didn't have the handcuffs. He asked me when Miss Belle had left, and I told him around four o'clock. He pulled a cigar from his pocket and just stood there giving me a hard look.

Finally, he lit his cigar, and after several puffs, he said, "What's a kid like you doing in a place like this?"

I said I was trying to make enough to go to Tyler Commercial College. That must have sounded funny to Lone Wolf, because he smiled for the first time.

"If I was you, young man, I would go there at the earliest opportunity."

As he turned to leave, I asked him.

"Sir, if it's not too much to ask, could I have your autograph?"

Lone Wolf stopped. "My what?"

"Your autograph, sir. I have this sheet of paper here."

Lone Wolf came back to my desk, laid down his cigar, and took the pen and wrote, "Manuel T. Gonzaullus, Sergeant, Texas Rangers."

The day Sam came back to get Miss Belle I left for Tyler. I didn't hear a word from either of them until the week of my graduation when Sam showed up in a big car wearing a diamond ring on his little finger. He said Miss Belle owned two honky-tonks and a lumber yard on the highway between Houston and Beaumont, and she wanted me to keep books for her when I graduated.

"No," I replied. "Tell her I said thanks. But I think not."

Stray Cats
and Free Enterprise

∽✑ ✑∽

In the thirties, Austin, Texas was still thought of primarily as a college town. The University, north of the Capitol, was a haven for the less than well-to-do who walked to class through alleyways infested with stray cats. Around the campus there were no parking lots, and you could ride the street car to the river south of the Capitol for a few pennies. Moonglow tower lights, much taller than ordinary street lights, combined beauty and economy, so they said. The tall towers seemed to reach for the stars, even at the bottom of the depression, and perhaps foretold Austin's destiny as the place of sophistication, traffic jams, and high-tech enterprise it is today. But for me, Austin will always be a city of impoverished students and stray cats.

I lived west of the campus on an alley where hordes of stray cats slunk up and down littered passageways, hopped up on garbage cans, ran in and out of empty garages, and made horrific cat love beneath the soft beams of the tower lights.

The garage under our room made a perfect cat rendezvous. Our landlady, Mrs. Grimes, often woke me up yelling, "Scat, you nasty cats!" She hated them. When I looked out, I could see her in curlers and a flannel bathrobe waving a worn-out broom at several scampering felines. One of these would be Tommie, a fluffy, white male who lured others into the empty garage below us for fighting or romancing, whichever was appropriate. Mrs. Grimes tried to keep Tommie out, but he could squirm beneath the locked doors through old tire ruts. I think Tommie knew my step. When I came home late in the day, he usually sauntered out of the garage to greet me. I didn't know whether I loved him as a playful clown or hated him as a lecherous fiend.

Hack, my roommate, who was called Haskell by his family, slept so soundly that he never heard the goings-on below until the cafe, where he waited on tables and where I typed menus, suddenly shut its doors for good. The day this happened, Hack came home late and went to bed hungry. That night, for the first time, he heard Tommie. He woke me up beating on the floor with his shoe and muttering something about strangling a few cats if he got hungry enough.

I turned on my light, got up, and went to my dresser.

"How about a Hershey?" I said.

Hack sat up in bed and squinted at the bar of chocolate I was holding out to him. He shook his head, then rolled over on his stomach and covered his head with his pillow.

I was rich but Hack didn't know it. That afternoon I had sold my Buescher True Tone trumpet down near the river for twenty dollars. I paid Mrs. Grimes eight dollars past-due rent and figured we could hold out until Hack collected his tutor's check. I also got on the waiting list for a part-time job in the Registrar's office during Thanksgiving and Christmas.

I tried again to rouse Hack.

"Up in Iowa, the government is paying farmers to kill little pigs and plow them under. Do you think we ought to call it quits and hitch up there? Wouldn't you prefer pig to cat meat?"

Hack got up without saying anything, then went into the bathroom and drank two glasses of water. He came out wiping his mouth on his hairy arm. His underwear shorts hung loose below his shrunken waist line. For a few moments he stood beside his bed with his back turned, staring down at the empty candy wrapper I had discarded. Then he turned around.

"I'm working on an idea," he said. "At Johns Hopkins they provide embalmed cats in the zoology labs instead of these god-awful vat specimens we use here. The students have to pay extra. I wrote off this afternoon for the specs on how to do it."

I sensed I was included in the plan, whatever it was. No need to ask questions--Hack would come out with the whole story soon enough--so I turned off my light and crawled under the covers.

I was dozing off when Hack called out, "We'll need some capital to get started. Maybe I can talk you into selling that goddam trumpet."

The next day Hack was waiting for me at noon outside my Latin class.

"Come on," he said. "I want to show you the lab."

As we were passing behind the kitchen of the new student commons, a black cat darted across our path. I stopped and spat three times to ward off the spell. Hack waited, impatient.

"Look," he said, "try to be rational for a few

minutes while I explain our deal. Another tutor knows I'm interested, and we've got to beat him to the punch. It's a sure thing unless the game gets too crowded."

He kept on talking as we climbed the steps of the zoology building.

"You just saw back there--stray cats are all over the place. Until we work down the population, they won't cost us anything."

Hack paused, waiting for me to say something.

"Don't you have any questions? Aren't you interested in making a buck? God knows, we'll need it."

Finally, a thought struck me, and I asked, "Who would buy a dead cat if you can't give away live ones?"

Hack seemed put out. "Can't you see they're worth more dead than alive? We'll offer a product that's clean, odorless, and long-lasting--one the student can work on in his room. They'll sell. I bet we can get three bucks apiece."

"Where will all this go on?"

"Right beneath our room. As close as a slaughterhouse to pigs in a cornfield."

That image horrified me but brought a smile to Hack's face as we proceeded down the hall to the lab. Hack opened the door. The odor was worse than the men's room at the railroad station.

Hack put on some rubber gloves, reached inside one of the vats, then tossed a naked, greenish form to me, hollering, "Here, Watson, catch!"

I caught the slimy thing in my bare hands. It smelled awful. I threw it into the vat, feeling sick to my stomach.

"See!" Hack shouted. "How much would you

pay not to have to touch a vat cat?"

As I washed my hands and arms, I wondered how pre-meds who treated cats like this could have any feeling for humans.

Mrs. Grimes liked the idea of ridding her garage of Tommie and his friends but thought a two-dollar monthly rental was too cheap. When Hack promised to double the rent after the first twenty-five cats, she caved in. She liked Hack. She called him a go-getter.

I had little stomach for the specifications when they arrived, but Hack studied them avidly. From our scanty resources, I bought formaldehyde, glycerin, and a five-gallon jug to mix them in. Hack brought yellow chromate, rubber hose, and a half-dozen hypodermic needles which he said he found in the zoo lab. Hack also made a pair of electrodes by cutting Mrs. Grimes's broom handle into two grip-sized sections and driving nails through them length-wise. He told her that in a week or two she wouldn't need her broom any longer.

On opening night, four cats, the maximum number we could handle at one time, lay quietly in burlap sacks on the dirt floor of the garage, and I stood guard over them with mounting dread while Hack made final preparations for the execution. I heard Tommie outside, complaining. Then I saw his paw beneath the door, followed soon by the tip of his nose. I kicked dirt in his face and pressed hard on his paw. He withdrew fast.

Hack had been watching, gripping his electrodes.

"The next time he tries that, grab him and put him in a sack."

As he was testing his electrodes one more time, making the sparks fly, a snarling, hissing cat fight sprang up under my feet. Tommie had crawled in unnoticed and had set upon one of the sacks. They were tumbling around in the dirt making an awful racket.

"Grab him and put him in a sack!" shouted Hack. Tommie worked me over, but I got him by the nape of the neck and flung him out.

"You ought to of put him in a sack," Hack complained.

"Maybe I will next time, but I'm going to buy some gloves first."

I lifted one of the sacks to the work bench and twisted the open end until the spine of the cat inside was bowed tightly against the closed end of the sack as described in the specifications. I closed my eyes and told myself that this cat we were about to electrocute was nameless, hungry, and homeless, with no prospects for improvement, and that perhaps we could be forgiven for taking his life in a good cause, cleanly and humanely. While I held the sack, Hack probed with his left-hand electrode until he found the base of the cat's spine. While holding the electrode in place, he located the other end of the spinal column with the right-hand electrode. Then he took a deep breath.

"You have a tight grip on that sack?"

"Yes."

"All right, here goes. Good-by, kitty." Then he pushed the right-hand electrode home.

The cat jerked rigid, lifting the sack, as the current realigned every neuron in its brain and spinal column. The sack grew tight but held. There was no sound, no odor, no escaping fluids. After three or four seconds, Hack released the right-hand electrode. The cat went limp immediately. Hack made contact again. The cat's body stiffened, but there was no sound.

Hack put away the electrodes as I dumped the lifeless cat onto the work bench, spread it out, and began tying its legs down. "Not too tight," Hack said. "The fluid has to penetrate the claws."

I had been dismayed just to read the procedures, but Hack had obviously memorized them. When I had the cat spread to satisfy him, Hack inserted a needle into the femoral artery of the cat's left hind leg and connected the needle to the rubber hose leading from the jug of embalming fluid mounted above the work bench. I pried open the cat's mouth and put a rubber stopper in it. As embalming fluid began flowing into the cat's body, we stepped back. After watching a while, I said, "It's really working." And Hack said, "What did you expect?"

A couple of nights later, when all four specimens were fully cured, I watched Hack remove the embalming needles and inject yellow chromate into the arterial system of each cat. This way, Hack said, the arteries would be yellow, the veins blue with coagulated blood, and the nerves white. With each specimen, we would provide a vial of embalming fluid for touching up dry spots and keeping the skin moist after the student peeled it back for dissection.

The demand for our specimens exceeded Hack's rosiest predictions. We sold ninety-seven cats and made a profit of seventy per cent. Mrs. Grimes was pleased when we doubled the rent and helped us cope with two checkers from the S. P. C. A.

Mrs. Grimes tipped us off, and the next night a man in suede gloves and a woman in a fur coat showed up. The man seemed affable enough, but the woman looked uncomfortable. Mrs. Grimes told them how we were getting rid of those pesky stray cats in such a clean way and so quiet about it she never heard a thing. She said she was only a poor widow woman doing the little bit she could to help the neighborhood, and that these boys were hard-working and honest as the day is long and would someday amount to something.

The woman didn't look at the specimens on cure when Hack lifted the cover, but the man did. He asked us how we held the cats while we electrocuted them. Hack showed him the electrodes and the hinged board he had recently added to hold down the twisted end of the sack. The man was leaning forward taking in every word, but the woman had her hand to her mouth as if she wanted to puke.

Just then Tommie wandered in, and I reached down to give his ear a scratch.

"Stanley," the woman whispered. "We should go. I've seen enough."

I guess she was afraid we might put on a demonstration, using Tommie as a specimen. As they were leaving, I thought how strange it was for anyone who wore animal skin to get so upset at the sight of a cat slaughterhouse.

During the spring semester, another group began embalming cats. The supply of strays dwindled, and we had to go down on the river and pay fifteen cents apiece for them to the little Mexican boys. Sometimes the street car conductor wouldn't let us on with our sacks, and we had to walk home. Regardless of these problems, we would probably have continued if I hadn't been so upset when Hack electrocuted Tommie.

It happened toward the end of the semester. I was working alone one night and was about to apply the electrodes when Tommie began nibbling at my ankles. Since I had my elbow on the hinged board to hold down the twisted end, I couldn't move far from the bench. I kicked at Tommie, and he backed off. But as I pushed the electrodes home, Tommie pounced and bit me hard. I didn't make good contact, the sack slipped, and the cat burst from the sack like a wild-eyed, four-legged ballistic missile. He began circling the walls, travelling so fast he barely touched a thing, and wailing like a fire engine. Coming toward the light from the dark corners, his eyes glowed like searchlights, and his tail stuck out like a bottle brush. Tommie had taken a stand in the middle of the floor, switching his tail and swivelling his head looking for an opening. Since I had no wish to tangle with an electrified cat, I opened the door. The stray shot through it like a streak of lightning and wailed off into the night.

Almost as a reflex, I reached down and picked up Tommie and thrust him into a sack. While twisting him up, I came to my senses, leaned over the work bench, and buried my face in my hands. Then Hack walked in, saw the twisted sack and the expression on my face and asked what the hell was going on. I told him, which was a mistake. Without a word, he picked up the electrodes and began maneuvering me out of the way.

"No! Haskell! No!" I shouted. But it was too late. Tommie's exit was already complete and final, and it no longer mattered whether I had loved or hated him.

Although we went in different directions, Hack

and I remained friends. He became a famous microbiologist and eventually returned to Austin, while I followed more ambiguous pursuits, one being to avoid alleys. I still shudder when I see a white, fluffy cat.

Hack is no longer impoverished. He was pulled into the vortex of high winds converging over Austin that are making it a center of high-tech enterprise, a type that appears to reduce risk to itself if not to outsiders. When I visit there, I am impressed and a little disturbed because I can't fully understand what Hack and his colleagues are saying or doing. I feel almost as ignorant as I imagine Tommie was when he tempted fate by lingering in our garage workroom. But I'm on guard. If I learned anything from working with strays, it is this: never let anyone pull a sack over your head, because if you do, you might wind up as a specimen.

Ringside Seat

∽◌ ◌∾

Just after World War II, I bought a house on Whisenant Street in a reclaimed swamp near Houston. Since my wife and I hadn't been married very long, the movers transported everything in their pick-up except our little dog and five watercolors. We took these in the car. The movers were waiting on the porch by the time we arrived. After they left, we sat down on packing boxes to cool off.

Our dog, Queequeg (we called him Queeks for short), was also taking a breather at our feet when he began whining. I heard a man's voice say, "Hello, anybody home?"

The fellow standing at the kitchen door reminded me of one of the Yucatan workmen we'd seen on our honeymoon. They were short, round, and usually bare to the waist. And very strong. Our visitor, although redheaded and freckled, had on yucatecan shorts which hid his knees but not his belly button. He held out two cans of beer and said, "Welcome to Whisenant Street. I'm Michael Francis Christopher Dooley. Call me Mike. I live next door."

I thanked him for the beer and introduced my

wife while Queeks sniffed at his bare feet.

Mike gave Queeks a nudge with his toe. "That's some dog. Where I go huntin' a critter that size would make just one bite for a bob-cat."

I expected Mike to stay, but he didn't. "Y'all come on over after awhile. Me and Rita'll be in the back."

After finishing the beer, we hung the watercolors, unpacked the boxes, and made the bed. Then we stopped to shower and change clothes.

Mike's house was on one side and a swampy vacant lot was on the other. The real estate agent had warned us not to let Queeks wander into the vacant lot because of snakes and big rats. A straggly hedge divided the narrow space between our two houses.

While we were dressing, my wife said our kitchens and bedrooms were so close together it was like being on stage.

We left Queeks at the kitchen door and stepped over the hedge into Dooley's back yard. Mike sat at a table littered with guns and knives, polishing what appeared to be a pair of brass knucks. A woman shorter than Mike, dressed in leotards, who had been lounging in a lawn chair, saw us first and stood up. She was thick in arm and thigh as if she had been taking body building exercises. Mike hopped up when he saw us and introduced us to his wife.

"This is Rita," he said. "We been married for as long as I can remember." He gripped her waist so tightly Rita squirmed. "She can't cook, but she can wrestle."

Rita bent one of Mike's fingers backward until he let go. Then she went across the yard for more chairs, moving like a squarely built ballet dancer.

When we were seated, I asked Mike about the weapons he was cleaning.

"I learned guns in the Marine Corps. I keep mine ready to go." Then he began an account of close combat with a Japanese. I tried to change the subject.

"Tell us about the brass knucks," I said.

Mike slipped a set on his fingers. "These belong to Rita. Her mother, old lady O'Reilly, gave them to her when we married and said she may need them to keep me in line. Being short on brains, she thought it was a cute stunt. I never held it against Rita. Did I, hon?" He went into a boxer's crouch and made feints at his wife.

That night, with all the bedroom windows open, we could hear every word Mike and Rita said. They were arguing about Rita's mother, Mrs. O'Reilly, who was coming for a visit. Mike objected to her travelling with a man who wasn't her husband. He said if she brought him along he would beat them both up. Before I drifted off to sleep, the idea of building a fence entered my mind.

The next day being Sunday, I slept until Queeks hopped up on our bed at eight o'clock, whimpering. I raised the blind and saw Mike wading in the vacant lot with a shotgun in the crook of his arm. He stopped, raised his gun, and fired. The blast tore a limb off a sunken log, and a snake fell into the water, tying itself in knots.

My wife sat up hollering Oh!, and Queeks ran in circles barking. I stuck my head out of the window and shouted, "Hey! What do you think you're doing!"

Mike slogged through the muck toward my window. When he got close, I asked him if he hunted snakes every Sunday.

"Every Sunday?" Mike parked his gun against my window and took off his boots. "Naw, not every Sunday. I didn't get to go huntin' this week-end, and I needed some practice." He squinted in the window. "You hunt?"

"No."

"I didn't think so." Then he walked away.

I called the Dooley's Friday night to tell them I was installing a fence for Queeks. Rita said fine. Mike had left on a week-end hunting trip.

While I was digging holes Saturday morning, Rita joined my wife in our back yard for iced tea. As they were chatting, I heard Rita say her mother and her uncle were coming soon. Uncle Robert, she said, was the youngest in the family and had been in poor health.

When Mike returned on Sunday afternoon he saw me and came over, stopping at the post between our kitchens. He stared at the line of posts.

"I can't believe it," he said. Then he grabbed the post and tried to shake it. I had set them in concrete.

Then he turned on me. "What do you think you're doin'! Look what you've done to my hedge!"

I explained I had been careful not to damage his hedge, but Mike wasn't listening. He grabbed the post again and gave it a hard tug. It didn't budge. Then he kicked it.

"This goddam post is on my property! I planted my hedge a foot inside the property line. You didn't check it. Nobody but a ribbon clerk would do a thing like this."

He stepped closer.

"A ribbon clerk!" he shouted. His breath was overwhelming. "You're nothing but a goddam ribbon clerk!" Then he turned and walked away.

The first thing Monday I engaged a surveyor. When I got home that evening I found him beside his van completing a plot plan of our two lots.

"I'm afraid the posts between the houses are all on the Dooley lot," the surveyor said. "But all the others are okay." As he was leaving, he said he would mail me some prints.

When the prints arrived I invited Mike over for a beer. As he studied the drawing, I offered to buy the few inches of his property I had encroached upon.

"Naw," he said, handing me the drawing, "you can buy me a case of beer. Old lady O'Reilly's coming Saturday and I can't stand to be around her. I'm goin' huntin'."

As I was nailing laths on the fence Saturday afternoon, a torpedo-back coupe with a cracked windshield creeped to a stop in front of Dooley's. Before the engine stopped coughing, a chunky little worman flung the door open and ran into the Dooley house. Then a bony-looking man got out, coughing like the car. After removing a suitcase from the trunk, he also went inside.

As my wife and I were eating supper, rain began to fall. Through the downpour, we could see Rita, Mrs. O'Reilly and "Uncle" Robert carrying on in the kitchen. Although Robert seemed to be having a good time, I heard him say he was all fagged out and wanted to turn in early, adding that he would be glad to sleep in the car.

"In this rain?" Mrs. O'Reilly cried. "No, siree! You'll sleep in the bed with me where you belong."

The rain was still coming down when my wife and

I retired. It was raining so hard I quit worrying about the wet paint on the fence and began worrying whether we should get out of our low area.

I was glad to see the rain had stopped when I took Queeks outside at midnight. As I waited, headlights turned into the Dooley driveway. Mike got out and left his headlights on. He looked drenched to the skin. I saw him throw a can of beer at Robert's car then go inside.

In no time at all, loud bumping and hollering broke loose next door. I could hear Mike yelling, daring Robert to come out and fight. Just then Robert appeared around the corner of the house running toward his car.

Meanwhile, Mike had come into the kitchen, shouting at Rita about tramps moving in the minute he turned his back. He took a beer out of the refrigerator then gathered up an armload of pots and pans and threw them outside. He took a swig of his beer then began raking dishes off the shelves onto the floor. Amid all the crashing and banging, he didn't hear Rita. She was wearing brass knucks on both hands. She planted a hard left on the kidney, then as Mike wheeled, she decked him with a right.

Mrs. O'Reilly helped Rita drag Mike to another part of the house, then Rita came back and began dialing. Mrs. O'Reilly followed. "Don't call the police!" she screamed. They wrestled until Mrs. O'Reilly slapped Rita so hard she dropped the phone and fell bawling to the floor.

When I got back to bed, my wife said she thought we ought to move.

The next morning, Robert's car was gone and Mike and Rita were sitting in the back yard reading the Sunday paper. Rita had a bandage over one eye. Mike was drinking beer through a straw and had a bandage that covered almost his entire head.

At that moment, I wasn't sure I wanted to move from Whisenant Street where the fights were so exciting and our kitchen and bedroom were the best seats in the house.

A Touching Example

⤳∽ ∽⤶

For most of my life, I've been a pencil-pusher struggling under mountains of paper, fighting a never-ending battle of fiscal deadlines, seeing the world through numbers, graphs, and charts. I have analyzed business operations without ever touching the machinery that made them go. My sense of touch has withered from lack of use. I knew I needed something I could get my hands on, like a small farm. After looking for a long time, I found a five-acre place with fruit trees and a tractor.

After we moved in, I took the tractor to Hugo, the neighborhood garageman, for a checkup. He disregarded the sluggish beat of the engine and the jumpy hitch of the transmission, but he said I should replace the rear tires.

"Them old rags is awful thin," he said, and gave one of the tires a kick. "I got a pair here, second-hand, for forty dollars. They oughta last as long as the tractor."

I agreed that the tires probably had an infirm grip on this world, but I said I wasn't planning to do anything with the tractor but plow the orchard.

"I was hopin' you wasn't gonna race with it," Hugo said.

I drove back to my place and spent the rest of the day plowing the orchard. The old tractor grunted up and down row after row all afternoon, and not once did I hear anything out of the ordinary. The buds on the trees were beginning to show color, a reminder that the former owner had told me to spray at pink bud and petal fall and three more times after that, two weeks apart. And so before calling it a day, I mixed the captan and malathion, hitched the spray tank to the back end of the tractor, and tested my hoses. The old tractor and I were all set for pink bud.

As I mounted the seat of the tractor the next morning, I noticed this swelling on the side of the left rear tire. It stuck out like an orange. I dismounted and began looking around for some tool, having no plan of what I'd do if I found one. Finally, I took my mechanical pencil from my shirt pocket and poked gently at the bulge.

The blast that followed blew off my cap and broke my glasses. With my hand over my injured eye, I hurried to the house where I upset my wife terribly when she saw the blood covering my face.

We made a quick trip to the doctor and learned that the blood came from a small cut in my eyelid. Since I wasn't really hurt, my wife suggested I drive the car home while she stayed behind and looked at draperies.

"On your way, you can pick up a can of linseed oil," she said. "The paint mixing instructions are on the counter by the kitchen stove. I'll ask the drapery shop lady to bring me home."

My wife was full of ideas about how to improve the looks of our place. She wanted me to paint the walls of the garage a special color, and she would paint chanticleer designs over that.

After picking up the linseed oil, I stopped at Hugo's garage and found him under a customer's car.

"I've come back for the tires, Hugo. Can you install them today?"

Hugo rolled himself out from underneath the car and squinted at me. He was built like a Japanese wrestler, only not so fat.

"What happened," he said. "You been in a wreck?"

"No, just a blow-out. The left rear."

Hugo rested his arms on his knees. Grease and sweat marked his shoulders.

"I've got to spray," I said. "It's pink bud."

Hugo sat like a Buddha. He seemed to be in deep thought. Then he laid himself back and rolled beneath the car. For a moment, I thought he was turning me down, then I heard him say, "Be out around two."

As soon as I walked into the kitchen, I saw the the paint mixing instructions on the counter. After locating my spare glasses, I began reading the instructions with my good eye. They said boiled linseed oil was required, and I had bought the plain.

Now, sometimes I read more into instructions than is intended or I trip on a trifling ambiguity others would ignore. I'm like a lint-picking lawyer, over-trained from reading so much boiler plate, such as the fine print on the back side of insurance policies. I object to a label which says, "Take one tablet twice a day." Doctors and pharmacists should say, "Take one tablet in the morning and another at bedtime." That would be longer, but it wouldn't be the least bit ambiguous.

I re-read the paint mixing instructions. The idea of boiling something that already looked well cooked seemed wrong to me, but there it was in black and white.

After pouring the linseed oil into a pot and setting the burner on medium, I went upstairs to change my blood-stained shirt. Then I looked everywhere for my notes on spraying. I finally found them and was on my way downstairs when I heard the door slam and my wife scream.

I came flying down the stairs and saw a sight only a few ever get to see. The linseed oil had overflowed onto the kitchen stove and had covered the paint mixing instructions with a thick layer of goo. As I stood there, a bubble formed around the rim of the pot. After it grew to the size of a child's balloon, it detached itself from the pot with a viscid smack, touched lightly on the vent-a-hood, and climbed the wall behind the stove, leaving grease spots all the way up.

My wife was screaming for me to do something, so I grabbed the pot handle. I stuck my finger in the goo to retrieve the instructions, but the stuff burned like fire and I dropped the pot. As the contents spread over the floor, the balloon burst on the ceiling, and some of the hot oil found its way down my neck.

I doctored my injuries myself this time, and later I retreated to the garage to get out of sight and to wait for Hugo.

I read my notes on spraying, looking for ambiguities. I didn't find any, but I was still uncertain. I needed more than visual confirmation. I needed a reliable sense of touch and a sixth sense I couldn't define, except to know that it was the one that judged the messages received from the other five.

I heard Hugo's truck before I saw it. The truck came down the lane at a crawl, and Hugo let it roll to a stop. He got out and went to the back end of his truck for the tires. Meanwhile, the engine continued to run, and after a last chug, there was a muffled backfire, as if Hugo had taught it manners.

Hugo saw me as he was jacking up the back end of the tractor. While twisting off the wheel nuts he asked me whether I had ever farmed before. I said I hadn't cultivated anything except a philodendron in my office downtown. He frowned but kept on working.

Hugo soon had the first wheel on the ground and was banging away with his sledge and levering the rim with a heavy tool. After a few more skillful knocks, he had the replacement on and the wheel remounted. As he began tightening the nuts, he said, "A farm ain't no place for somebody who can't use his hands. You need a few lessons."

He finished the second wheel and began putting his tools in the back end of his truck. Looking at the check I handed him, he said, "If someone came to me real serious about learning how to fix things, I wouldn't mind letting him watch me, if he stayed out of the way."

Then he climbed in his truck and waved good-bye.

Sinister Dominance

One morning I read an article about a computer science professor who said he'd been under the domination of the left side of his brain for so many years that he'd almost worked himself to death. The professor, who was in his fifties, had just undergone triple-by-pass surgery to correct the damage done by stress and overwork. He blamed everything on the left side of his brain. And then he said something I had to read twice. By looking at ourselves from the right side of our brains, he said, we can become more intuitive, less driven, and better balanced as we grow older. The potential for self-improvement is fascinating, he maintained.

Before I quit working, I'd had visions of someday sitting around doing nothing in that blissful state called retirement. But after I retired, life didn't go as I'd expected. I dreaded for someone to ask, "And what are you doing these days?" because I felt so guilty being idle. I found I could throw away my alarm clock but I couldn't get rid of my inner clock. I yearned for that time when I'd automatically gotten up at six-thirty, bathed and shaved, eaten breakfast, then gone downtown. I missed the piles of letters and the demands of the telephone.

And so, to get away from the house, I began to spend hours at the stockbroker's mindlessly watching the tape. I also kept logs of trips, visits, rainfall, sunrise, and sunset. I mowed the grass more frequently, I shined my shoes when they didn't need it, and I did chores I'd never done before, like waxing floors and cleaning out closets. (I couldn't sit idle and watch the clouds go floating by; I had to stay busy doing something, no matter how trivial.) But now, I suddenly realized that, if the professor knew what he was talking about, I could still be under the domination of the left side of my brain, and I might therefore be robbing myself of that vision I'd had of my retirement years.

The article said the professor--and the surgeon who'd operated on his heart--were appearing that evening at a local hospital in a public presentation. I almost dismissed the impulse to go, then I caught myself. Did the impulse come from the right side of my brain and was my left side trying to stifle it?

That night the meeting in the hospital auditorium was well attended, mostly by people my age. There was also a scattering of young interns, in white. On the stage sat two men: the surgeon in a white smock, and the professor in a turtle-neck shirt and jacket. The surgeon looked sound as a dollar to me, but there was something odd in the way the professor kept his eyes closed as if in meditation.

In his introduction, the surgeon said he was grateful that his operation on the professor had turned out so well. Then he began reviewing some of the familiar evidence of the brain's left-side functions. He said he wasn't sure dominance was the right word. Because of the criss-cross in the nervous system, the left side of the brain controlled the muscles of the right side of the body and appeared to be dominant because it also controlled speech. He was sure most people in the audience had seen the results of stroke on the left side of the brain.

He went on to mention that circulatory problems like the professor's were aggravated by stress. And he concluded by saying that the medical profession had found out how to treat stress but didn't know much about the imbalance associated with it. Then he sat down.

The professor got up, removed his jacket, and went to the rear of the platform where he did a handstand. I thought to myself, this man is going to be just another yogi. While his face turned red, the professor said that the imbalance the surgeon referred to is rooted in the opposing sides of the brain. In a world ruled by communications, the left side has become dominant, and this dominance, he said, is augmented by the analytical, sequential, and rational characteristics of the left side, as contrasted to the creative, intuitive, and non-sequential qualities of the right side. What is needed, he said, is a proper balance between the two sides for good health and a positive attitude toward life. If the imbalance continues into later life, a person's undesirable personality traits may dominate the gentler ones.

As I listened, I studied the surgeon's face, trying to discern whether he was going along with the professor. He appeared neutral, and he didn't seem surprised when the professor flipped himself right side up. The audience, probably as uncertain as I, gave the professor some restrained applause.

In the question-and-answer period that followed,

the professor told about solving certain problems in his computer work which had baffled him in the past. He said he did it with an intuitive insight which had been stifled by his relentless work habits before the operation. What is important is to maintain balance. Only then will our creative and intuitive selves have a chance.

That night, as I lay awake, I turned the professor's ideas over in my mind. One part of my brain said the whole performance was ridiculous, but the other part said, Don't forget the surgeon--he sat through it and kept a straight face. The controversy in my head was like two people arguing. The argument went on until I decided to name the one taking the professor's side Dexter, and the one against him Sinister. Dexter wanted Sinister to take a fresh point of view, and after a while, I heard Sinister say, "Shut up, Dexter. I'm trying to think."

"You call that thinking?" Dexter said. "That one-plus-one-equals-two type of cerebration?"

"Can you do any better?"

"Not better, just easier and less frantic. The professor says that since we're retired, we don't have to be in such a hurry any longer. We have time to look out of the window and dream."

"You're just lazy," Sinister snapped. "I'd feel guilty if we weren't busy."

"All you do is go around in circles. You keep up a pretense of working so you won't have to look at yourself. And where has all that busy, busy work got us?"

"Pretty far," argued Sinister. "We've made enough to retire on. What's more, I can still be useful and productive. I know a lot of things you don't. I understand the jargon of business, economics, and finance, and I'm learning computer-speak. And what can you do? You can't say a word without running it through me."

"Yeah, and you get it all garbled."

I got out of bed, went into the kitchen and heated a cup of water in the microwave. As I stirred in the decaf, I asked myself, Am I in balance? Do I have intuition? Is my personality becoming skewed?

I didn't drink my coffee. Instead, I closed all the blinds, took off by bedroom slippers and tried to do a handstand against the wall. I tried again and again. Finally, I gave up and stretched out on the floor. I felt giddy, and I was breathing hard. I kept listening for voices but none came. Clearly, it would take time to get outside myself, but I would keep trying. After all, another me was hiding in there somewhere. I had heard it, even though the dominant me tried to garble it. I wanted to hear it loud and clear.

Accounting
for
Females

As soon as the plane landed, I took a taxi directly to the campus. The dean would be gone for the day, but Miss Hardy, his Administrative Assistant, would still be there. Lori Hardy and I had been in the same business letter writing class twenty-five years ago.

Since then the campus had grown enormously-- more buildings and more students, especially women. On my last recruiting visit, the number of women taking accounting subjects had multiplied ten times. Our firm was hiring more women all the time, but not all of my partners agreed, especially Blake, a bachelor, who said that if lawyers and accountants finally inherited the earth, as the saying goes, then the ruling class would be primarily women.

The dean's office was still in the old building with the statue of the Roman god Mercury in front. The statue always brought to mind what one of my professors said: accounting is an art, not a science. I felt at home here, even though most of my professors had retired.

Lori was in conference when I arrived. The male receptionist (Lori always put a good-looking fellow out front) said I was expected and would I like to see a profile of the graduating class while waiting?

I sat down to read the catalog he handed me. According to it, seventy percent of the top quartile of students taking accounting subjects were women. Blake could be right for a reason he would not like: maybe women were better suited to accounting than men.

The door to Lori's office swung open, and Lori came striding out. She graduated summa cum laude and had never married. Although she was not an accounting major, our firm wouldn't have hired her in those days even if she had been. We believed then as Blake still believed that woman's place was in the home and that she was just terrible at math.

Lori shook hands quickly. "Sorry to keep you waiting. The computer breaks down at the end of every semester, it seems. How are you?"

"Fine, Lori, and you are, too, obviously."

As we sprinted to her office, I commented upon the number of women taking accounting, and she said, yes, in the old days male professors complained how their "boys" went into the business world and were soon drawing salaries as large as theirs. "Now their female students are doing the same thing," she said, thrusting an interview schedule at me.

Maybe she believed most men felt envious of women. But I saw nothing wrong with men being paid as much as women for the same work.

Attached to the schedule was another sheet showing the grades of the top ten students. Lori put check marks by three names, one of which was a woman, Verna Mae Dawson. Then she drew a red line through one of the men's names. I noted that his grades were excellent.

When I looked up, Lori said, "You don't want him." Then she explained that the campus police had caught him flashing last week near one of the women's dorms.

"First offense?" I said.

"Who knows?" Lori said, not smiling.

I thought of Lori passing the statue of Mercury every morning on her way to work. It was a beautiful figure of a man in a state of permanent flash. Did she notice it? Did she pay any more attention to her male receptionist? Lori's conservative suit reminded me that dress codes permit women to be quasi-flashers in social gatherings but not at work.

Lori was standing to let me know it was time to go. I would have loved to invite her to dinner, but she would decline, saying there were too many other recruiters on campus who might think she was playing favorites.

That night, after a long-distance talk with the managing partner of our firm, it was agreed that I should hire the woman, Verna Mae Dawson, if she looked half as good on foot as she did on paper, then settle for any two of the men in the top ten, except the flasher, of course. The managing partner got a bang out of the flasher story and said he ought to ask Blake if he had ever done any flashing.

"What about Blake?" I said. "He told me we're getting too many women on the staff."

"I'll take care of Blake," the managing partner said.

Verna Mae's grades were more pleasant to look at than her face. Her teeth stuck out so far she had trouble hiding them.

"Why did you choose public accounting as a career?" I asked her.

"Because I like accounting. It's easy for me. And law is too slow. It would take too long."

"You don't have any law courses on your record."

"No, there was only enough money for four years."

"Would you object to travel?"

"Not at all. I understand my living expenses would be paid when I was traveling. Is that right?"

"Yes, as long as you're doing work for a client."

I could hear Blake saying he wouldn't allow anybody with teeth like that on any of his jobs, in town or out.

"You seem to have A's in just about all your subjects. Which ones do you like best and least?"

"I like taxes best, then computer science. Auditing didn't really appeal to me. But I'm sure I could do it."

"Do you have a brother or sister here?"

"No. I have no family at all. My aunt raised me and she's dead."

I thought of Lori, who was the youngest of many children in her family. The last time I asked, she was still living with her parents. Would the university have hired her if she had had teeth like Verna Mae's?

"Miss Dawson, would you tell me where you expect to be ten years from now?"

Verna Mae was ready for that one. Without hesitating, she said she expected to be a partner in a large accounting firm or operating a firm of her own.

A person has to have superior intelligence just to

comprehend the morass of laws and regulations in taxes, and to be a star, he has to see himself as a duelist in a fight to the finish with the government. All of us were astonished that Verna Mae could be as deadly in battle as a man. She hit the government with thousands of dollars of claims. She also found errors that had been repeated on certain tax returns for years, and thus she caused the firing of two senior male accountants in the height of the tax season when the department worked around the clock and could least afford to lose anybody. After the peak was over, she had braces put on her teeth and then proposed that we computerize our returns.

The only computer in town large enough to handle our volume was at Bruner Manufacturing Company, a non-client we had drooled over for years. Waldo Streicher, the Controller, who had been Blake's friend since boyhood, said he would be glad to rent us his spare capacity, provided we would let that female tax demon make a tax survey of his company at no charge.

Although Blake had always considered Bruner Manufacturing his personal bailiwick, we made a deal with Waldo while he was away for the summer teaching at his alma mater. On the day Blake returned from teaching, Verna Mae, Waldo and I were reviewing her report on Bruner Manufacturing's tax picture in Blake's office.

Blake didn't recognize Verna Mae; he was so surprised to see Waldo he didn't even take off his hat. After a while, I said, "Blake, you remember Miss Dawson, don't you?"

He shook her hand, obviously uncertain who she was.

Verna Mae no longer wore braces at the office. I supposed she wore them at night, because her teeth looked much better, and her figure was filling out. She was also going steady with a young tax lawyer named Tony, whom we met one night at Verna Mae's after a play. Later, my wife said the relation between Verna Mae and Tony looked serious to her.

"I'm sorry we've messed up your office, Mr. Blake," Verna Mae said. "It'll take only a minute to clear all my stuff out after our meeting."

"I don't see why that's necessary," Waldo interrupted. "Anybody who can be gone three months without being missed obviously doesn't need an office."

I laughed and Verna Mae turned pink.

Blake finally took off his hat. "Oh, that's who you are--Miss Dawson, of course. I didn't recognize you."

Blake hung his hat on the costumer, then turned and faced us. "Well, will somebody tell me what's going on here?"

Waldo patted Verna Mae's shoulder. "This little lady is the fastest rising tax expert in town, Blake. You'd better give her a big raise before somebody hires her away from your firm."

As soon as Waldo left, Blake barged in on the managing partner and threatened to split the firm if Verna Mae stayed on the staff. After they had argued back and forth, the managing partner asked me to talk to him, but it was like insisting that we keep a flasher on the payroll. In a few days, Verna Mae came to me for advice.

"I hadn't planned to leave this soon," she said, "but I think I'd better reconsider."

"Don't do anything rash, Verna Mae. Blake will cool off in a month or so. We've got some plans for you that will keep you interested and out of Blake's way."

"There's something else. You met Tony. He wants to marry me."

"Congratulations! He seemed like a fine young man. But that's not grounds for leaving the firm. We don't operate that way."

"I know, but you see, I'm pregnant."

"Oh, well."

Verna Mae suddenly seemed vulnerable. I thought she really did want my advice.

"That makes it even easier," I said. "A temporary leave would be just the thing. Then after the baby arrives, you can come back and pick up where you left off. By that time, Blake will have forgotten the whole thing."

Verna Mae is now in her seventh month, waiting. Meanwhile, Blake seems to be softening. If he returns to normal, I might ask him to go recruiting with me soon. I want him to meet Lori. Maybe they'll discover how much they need each other.

Managing is Fun

Soon after I was hired at Mr. Selensky's meat-packing plant, I asked Hudgins, the canned ham product manager, about his inventory shortages. Hudgins said he had tried to find the answer but couldn't get anywhere with Smrz, the canning and boning foreman.

So I made a special trip to the plant. Smrz said Hudgins hadn't been in his right mind since Mr. Selensky had fired him for alcoholism when he was general sales manager then re-hired him as canned ham product manager, but only--and Smrz seemed to enjoy telling this--after Hudgins came crawling back, begging for a job. Smrz also asked me why the front office didn't let Knuth worry about the shortages. If someone was stealing, Knuth was the one to catch them.

Setting aside Smrz's impertinence for another time, I asked my secretary to set up a meeting with Hudgins, Smrz, and Knuth in my office on Monday afternoon at four.

As I was parking Monday morning, the main gate guard came over to my car lugging a basket of fresh tomatoes and a bucket of okra. He wanted to know whether I would be so kind as to set them in Mr. Selensky's office.

"Sure," I said. "Who brought them?"

"Two of them DP's. One was Smrz," the guard said, hurrying away to a truck standing at the main gate.

I wrote it off as a coincidence that Smrz made the deliveries when he did. Since June, I had seen baskets of corn, beans, okra, and tomatoes delivered to Mr. Selensky's office from the vegetable garden at the north end of the plant property, which some DP's still cultivated.

The DP's, ("Displaced Persons") were a group of over two hundred families whom Mr. Selensky had rescued from European detention camps, chartering a ship and bringing them to jobs at his plant after World War II.

The plot of ground which Mr. Selensky had turned over to the DP's for a vegetable garden had been the livestock truck parking lot, and because of the drippings out of the trucks, it was the most fertile area of the plant property. The old north-end livestock gate was still there, but it was kept locked because all livestock trucks now entered through the south gate. All other traffic used the present main gate. At this location, long eighteen-wheelers barely cleared the railroad tracks when they stopped for check-out. But Mr. Selensky refused when I asked him to have the gate moved to the north-end site. He said trucks were getting too long, anyway. When he made remarks like that, I marveled at his success in business.

At three o'clock, Mr. Selensky came into my office wanting to know why I was having a meeting with Smrz. I considered asking him who told him about the meeting, but instead I held out a copy of the canned ham shortage report. "Have you seen this? Knuth and Hudgins are also coming. Would you like to join us?"

"You're wasting your time," Mr. Selensky said. "Let Knuth handle shortages. We don't have any theft in this plant because everybody knows they'll be fired immediately if they're caught. What this plant needs is more sales effort, not lint-picking." He turned and went back into his office without glancing at the shortage report.

Knuth was in charge of plant security and the guards at the main and south gates. He was on duty himself from sunset to sunrise. With a massive key ring chained to his belt, he roamed in and out of the many buildings which extended for almost a mile along the railroad tracks. It seemed to me that Knuth had the greatest opportunity of all to steal.

Hudgins came in first. He was a large man with bulging eyes that darted in every direction as though he expected to find a ghost hiding somewhere.

"Tell me about Knuth," I said, closing the door. "Is he a DP?"

"Yes, sir." Hudgins shifted his glance from the window to my telephone and tapped a cigarette on his thumbnail in an unconscious way.

"What do you know about him?"

"Not much, sir. Mind if I smoke?" Hudgins's eyes focused on mine briefly, then shifted to his cigarette lighter. He told me Knuth's wife had worked in the plant lard refining laboratory but was now a buyer for a hotel chain. "She buys our bacon and salami, but not our hams," he said, lifting his eyes.

According to Hudgins, Knuth went out into a blizzard and rescued the old man--as he called Mr. Selensky--after Selensky had tried to reach the plant on foot during the storm.

Then Hudgins lowered his voice and leaned forward, "If you want my opinion, sir, I think Smrz and Knuth are in cahoots, although Knuth is more like a Nazi than a DP. The old man thinks they're loyal, but I think they're stealing him blind. Everyone thinks so, but they're afraid to talk.

"Do you have any proof?"

"No, sir. I've watched all night at a window in the motel across the tracks from the canning building but never saw anything."

The door cracked and my secretary said Knuth and Smrz were here. She stood back and Knuth rushed in ahead of Smrz and stuck out his hand.

"Sorry if I kept you waiting, sir. I was checking baskets and lunch buckets of first shift people leaving the plant. Just letting them know we're watching, sir, if you know what I mean."

Smrz, glaring at Knuth, slumped into a chair, but Knuth and Hudgins waited until I sat.

Turning to Knuth, I said, "I understand you're familiar with the canned ham shortage problem. Do you have any suggestions?"

Knuth crossed his arms and snorted. "I'm outta ideas on Smrz's shortages. To my mind, you'll spend more money trying to find a small shortage like that than it's worth."

"Do you think it's an inside job?"

"I don't have the least notion, sir."

"Maybe somebody's hauling them out that old north gate when the guard isn't looking," Smrz said.

Knuth turned and shouted, "More likely those DP vegetable farmers are taking them home in their baskets under all that corn and okra!" In a milder tone, he said, "Besides, my guards are trained to watch everything."

The next day I told my secretary and Mr. Selensky I was going to hide out for a few days in the motel across the tracks from the canning building. Mr. Selensky objected, saying I should be spending the time in New York or Chicago working with sales. But I went anyway.

During the long nights at the motel, I looked forward to the thunderous interruptions of the trains. There was a north-bound freight about one-thirty, and later, another one going in the opposite direction.

Shortly after my seventy-second hour, when I was beginning to think Mr. Selensky was right, I saw the headlight of the approaching one-thirty freight and heard the blast of the diesel locomotive. I could see the guard waiting outside his kiosk at the main gate crossing, and I watched him wave to the engineer until the pounding locomotive blocked my view.

A few big trucks left the plant during the next hour, headed for eastern markets, and a trio of workers from the all-night shipping department dashed across the tracks during their break for a fast beer. They soon returned, running to beat the oncoming south-bound freight which had just blasted its horn for the crossing. The guard was waving them across when I saw Knuth.

He was pushing a fully loaded cart from the canned ham building toward the north gate which was wide open. He got through the gate, but one of the cart wheels stuck in a hole just as the south-bound locomotive blocked my view.

I bolted from the room and got outside before the train passed. After the last car roared by, I ran across the tracks. Knuth didn't see me coming.

"Good morning, Knuth," I said. Is that a rush order?"

He spun around, obviously startled, then leaned against the load of canned hams.

"No, sir," he said. "I found this cart stuck. Whoever was trying to steal it must have run off."

"How do you suppose he got a key to the north gate?"

Knuth looked down and ran the keys through his fingers.

"That's a real mystery to me, sir."

"Well, if you can't answer that I guess you'd better hand over your keys. You know the rules. You can come in Friday for your check."

Knuth said nothing. He took the key ring off the chain and handed it to me. Then he walked across the tracks and disappeared.

I yelled to the guard at the main gate to help me with the cart. He acted surprised but didn't ask me what I was doing at the plant at this hour.

When we finished with the cart, I fired him too.

Hog Heaven

When I signed on as treasurer of a meat packing company, I didn't know that two qualified people had turned down the job, nor that the company had stopped recruiting in business schools for the simple reason that too few showed up for the interviews. The personnel director gave me a questioning look and said that many financial people were too squeamish to work in a meat packing plant. Trying to sound confident, I replied that I hadn't been worried since seeing the company's humane slaughter award in the reception room.

During my first week, the president of the company invited me on a plant tour. I made a lame excuse because I planned to take a tour by myself. Were the sights and sounds in the plant as bad as I'd heard? How would I react to seeing pools of blood and hearing the squeals of animals? The place to begin, from what I had read in my procedure manual, was in the live end, which meant the stockyards and the upper floor of the kill building.

Later, I stopped at the supply room for a white butcher's smock which was required to be worn in the plant by visitors, supervisors, and office personnel. The laundry had pressed this smock so hard that the supply clerk had to help me separate the sleeves from the rest of the garment. Furthermore, hard launderings had left faint patterns in the fabric from prior blots and spatterings. I wished the smock had been red in the first place.

With a helmet on my head and my procedure manual under my arm, I went forth. I marched past a long row of multi-storied structures where routine factory operations like ham canning, bacon slicing and sausage making took place. These types of activities were dull compared to what I'd heard about the live end. If I could hold my own there, the rest would be easy.

When I arrived at the stockyards, a sharp wind was blowing, and the hogs were huddled in small groups keeping warm. Neutered males, called barrows, and unbred females, called gilts, were sleeping together in layers, unaware how short life was in the live end. Some groups had red hair, some white, some black, and others had a combination of colors. They seemed so content. But I reminded myself that they were placed on earth to serve man and that meat packers performed a needed service.

Upon entering the stockyards office, I introduced myself to the hog buyer and thought I saw an amused glint in his eye when he glanced at my procedure manual. He had little time to talk. His office overlooked the weight scale, and a radio crackled continuously reporting prices being paid for livestock. We watched a drover below us weighing a lot of hogs as they stood on tip-toe on the scale.

I had read in the manual that hogs don't like to

walk on hard surfaces because they have no heels. Their insides, though, are remarkably similar to human insides. This bothered me. If I were going to watch things happen to fish or chickens, I wouldn't have minded nearly so much.

When the weighing was done, the buyer made out a ticket and put it in the vacuum tube for the trip to the office. In a few minutes, the check came back the same way.

As another batch of hogs came down the wide central alley from the distant end of the stockyards, I asked the buyer why the unloading chutes hadn't been placed closer to the scale. This time I was sure he was amused as he described what hogs do as soon as they touch ground after a long truck ride. He added that the hog alley could be paved in gold with the money saved in this manner.

Through another window in the buyer's office, I saw drovers prodding batches of hogs into an elevator in the adjoining kill building and knew where the elevator was taking them. I could hear their squeals but I didn't think the drovers were hurting them. Declining an invitation to ride up with a batch, I climbed the stairs, clutching my manual. But the time for reading about what happened on the upper story of the kill building was over. I was now face to face with the real thing.

Dreading what I was about to witness, I stood outside the room called the stick room and listened. Hearing only faint sounds, I pushed it open and found myself in bedlam.

Continuous squealing, like a dozen sirens, bounced off the concrete walls of the room. It came from the hogs who were being prodded from the elevator onto a moving restrainer. As soon as they were locked in place, a stunner tapped them with his electric probe. Then they stopped squealing.

The unconscious hogs slid one at a time off the restrainer onto a stainless steel conveyor which carried them to the sticker waiting at the end of the line with his wide-bladed knife. He stood in a pool of blood, bare to the waist, with more blood dripping from his rubber apron.

Although the air in the room was warm with the heat of animals and thick with the odor of their blood, I didn't feel sick; the scene was too intense.

A hog lying prone on the conveyor approached the sticker with his throat in full view. The sticker was aiming his knife at the exact spot on the hog's throat that he wanted to pierce. As the blade slid in, the sticker's face tightened into a Mephistophelean smile. When he withdrew his blade, blood splashed his apron and thereafter surged in dwindling spurts to the last beats of the animal's heart, finally ebbing to a trickle. With smooth precision, the sticker looped a chain around the hog's hind leg, and his muscles bulged as he lifted the hog high enough to hook the loop to a conveyor. After the hog was whisked away, the sticker wiped his blade on his apron and turned to deal with the next creature giving his all for the benefit of mankind.

Suddenly, the squealing stopped, and I saw that the stunner had run out of live hogs. Three inert hogs lay on the conveyor moving toward the sticker. After they had been stuck, bled, and whisked away, the only sound in the room came from blood gurgling down the drain. It was then the sticker glanced at me. His half-grin must have meant he was amused by my looks, but I didn't feel sick, just weak in the knees.

Returning his smile as best I could, I bowed my way out and closed the heavy door behind me. I stood there for a minute thinking of the sticker. He seemed to take such pride in his work, but how on earth could he eat meat?

I took it slow on the way to the carcass dressing area. It was big, noisy, and filled with a refreshing odor of pine tar. A hundred people worked on a hundred hog carcasses suspended from a moving conveyor line which thumped along like a slow freight train. For a better view, I climbed up on a platform above a tank where the hogs soaked before they entered a rotating drum called a dehairing machine.

The smell of tar was helping a lot. As the hogs fell onto a table from the dehairing machine, a man inserted gambrels in the tendons of the hind legs of each carcass. Then the conveyor swept the hogs off the table and plunged them head first into a pit filled with hot tar. The conveyor immediately yanked them out of the pit so the hot tar wouldn't scorch their skin. Then a team of bare-waisted men stripped off the rapidly hardening tar. When the last blemishes had been removed by scrapers, the white-skinned hogs, as naked as the day they were born, were carried to the line of workmen waiting with their knives, cleavers, saws, gouges and machetes.

Just then I saw the president coming but he didn't see me on the lofty platform. He stopped to talk to the superintendent. After they exchanged a few words, the superintendent hurried away.

The president walked over to the conveyor line and spoke with the workman who was pulling tissue that lined the rib cage of each carcass. I learned later this tissue was called leaf lard and that removing it was one of the hardest jobs on the line. I saw the workman bow, hand his gloves to the president and step back. Then my boss put on the gloves and an apron and began pulling leaf lard.

In a few minutes, the superintendent returned with an arm load of dahlias. The president removed his gloves and took the flowers in his arms. After a few more words, he waved to everyone and left.

When I returned to the office, I saw the giant bouquet. My secretary told me that the superintendent raised dahlias as a hobby and that the president went down to the carcass dressing floor about once a month to pull leaf lard. "Just to remind himself where the money comes from," my secretary said.

I was beginning to realize that those two people who turned down the treasurer's job had done me a real favor. Seeing a sticker with such skill and having a boss who pulled leaf lard told me I had come to the right place.

Eager Beaver

Danny, a successful car dealer I knew in Salt Lake City, came by my office one day and said, "I'm starting a new line; I'm going to raise Canadian beaver, and I want you as my partner."

He explained how a matched pair of beaver had the capability of producing offspring in such quantities that the multiplying generations would make me rich before I was forty. "And I know you like to make a buck," he said. (I thought I hid it better than that.)

"How much investment are you talking about?" I asked.

"Five thousand for a pair, plus a hundred a month for looking after them in the pens on my ranch."

"How much did they cost you?"

"The same." He showed me an invoice from a Canadian outfit for three pair--fifteen grand.

"Look at this chart," he said. "In five years, you'll own eighteen beaver, assuming two kits to the litter. In just three more years, you'll own fifty!"

In my head, I multiplied fifty times twenty-five hundred and got a hundred and twenty-five thousand. After room and board, that would still be an interesting figure.

"It looks as if you've assumed each pair born will be a male and a female."

"Yes. That may be a weakness," Danny said. "Beaver don't usually switch mates, so more females than males wouldn't necessarily improve the production rate. On the other hand, there can be as many as eight in a litter. The average is four, and some females will have a second litter in August, sometimes."

"How can you be sure of the sex so as to match them?"

"That's easy." Danny pulled an envelope out of his pocket and laid six photographs on the table. They looked like little X rays.

"These are pictures of the genitals of the three pairs: Howard and Jane, Bill and Sue, and Bob and Mary. Do you see that little white streak in each boy's picture? That's his penis bone. When the time comes, I'll have the kits x-rayed so we can match them up."

"I never heard of raising beaver in pens before. Has it been tried?"

"Not around here. Beaver don't do well in captivity. But with good care, I think we can encourage them to breed as they do in the wild state."

"But that could be a major problem."

"Yes."

"Assuming you lick the breeding problem, where would we sell them?"

"To guys like you who know how much a mink coat is worth and can see that beaver fur is richer and deeper than mink fur. Beaver fur is waterproof. Another thing. Five grand is cheap when you think of the tax advantages."

"Not if we can't find guys crazy enough to pay twenty-five hundred apiece."

"If we can't peddle them as breeding stock, we can always sell them to pelters at lower prices."

Danny laid down a bill of sale listing the three pair: Howard and Jane, Bill and Sue, Bob and Mary.

"Look, if you want to think it over, take until tomorrow. Or just tell me you're not interested and I'll get somebody else."

"No. Wait a second."

This wasn't just a high-risk deal. It was insane. But the potential was so big I couldn't resist it. I selected Bill and Sue; then I wrote a check.

"Thanks very much. Don't worry. You've made a good investment. I'll pick you up Saturday morning and take you out to see Bill and Sue."

After he left, I wondered why I hadn't asked whether my pair had ever had a kit before.

At the ranch Saturday morning, we went inside a narrow building where twelve closet-size concrete pens were strung out below a walkway. Water flowed from pen to pen through mesh too hard even for beaver teeth, Danny said.

Each of the occupied pens had two name tags. After locating Bill and Sue, I asked Danny which was which, and he told me I would have to wait until one of them got pregnant. The larger one, whom I decided to call Bill, must have weighed fifty pounds, and at that moment he was moving his jaws sidewise making an awful grating sound.

"Sharpening his teeth," Danny said. "Their teeth never stop growing."

When I remarked how clean the pens were, he said that beaver went to the bathroom in the water and had sex there too. But he'd never seen them do it.

Bill was sitting up, dipping something green with his paw from an opening between his hind legs, then eating it.

"Look! He's eating that horrible green stuff.

"Danny called it digested cellulose. "It's the same as a cow chewing her cud. It comes out down there through an opening some people call a cloaca. Both sexes have one, and it's where everything else comes out. The mating organs are anterior, you see. That's why some say beaver mate front to front."

And I had thought humans were the only animals who made love like that.

I walked from the pens into what Danny called the greenhouse, where I saw a pile of green sticks in one corner and corn growing in a vertical rack of trays.

Soon after that first visit, I began feeding Bill and Sue myself. At first they stayed in the water the whole time. Eventually they began to recognize me, I think. After eating, they groomed each other. They dug deep into the fur with their front paws (Danny called them hands) and combed it with the double claws on their hind feet. Sometimes they dived into the water, then shot upward, slapping their tails on the surface, making sounds like rifle shots.

Once, Bill came out of the water and began roaming around the pen. He paused at a pile of gnawed sticks in one corner. Suddenly, he squatted, made some grunting noises, and left a reddish brown deposit over the sticks. Danny said Bill was putting down castoreum.

"That means he's staked out this territory as his

own."

"Where does the stuff come from?"

"It's secreted by two big glands, one on each side of the cloaca. Each gland is as big as my fist. In the old days, Indians used castoreum as a cure-all for almost everything except bringing the dead back to life."

In a little while, Sue also made a tour, discovered Bill's deposit, and added some of her own.

Months went by, and when March came with no signs of pregnancy, Danny put Howard and Jane into a tank. They immediately began cutting down small trees and building a lodge on the bank. Danny said they would dig one or more tunnels from the bottom of the tank to a dining room above water level inside the lodge.

August came and went, but still no kits. Not even Howard or Jane showed any signs. Danny wouldn't admit being discouraged, but he was avoiding me. The hundred dollars a month was becoming tiresome, and I said so.

"Why don't we close up shop and see if the people you bought these neuters from will give us a refund.?"

"Oh, no! We can't do that," Danny said. "I've got it all worked out. Look at this ad."

I took the single sheet Danny handed me and read:

Danny Deaver, the successful auto dealer, is off on a new tangent. He asserts that as the result of a forthcoming marketing campaign, a new product, Beaverol, will soon be found in more than half the households of the city. People of all ages will be demanding it for

*headaches, pimples, halitosis, dandruff, falling
hair, constipation, splitting fingernails,
tennis elbow, diarrhea, lagging sex performance,
and a host of other ailments.*

Now I knew Danny was adrift and headed for the
shoals. I told him to count me out; he could have Bill
and Sue and I would stop paying the hundred a
month.

Later, I read where Danny skipped out, boarding
a freighter for a trip around the world.

A year passed; then I got a letter from him from
New Guinea. He said he had a job in inter-tribal
tournaments held every month in a remote region;
he was one of the prizes awarded in the women's
competition. It was fun, he said, but he was feeling
weak. "Ship me some Beaverol. I hid a hundred
cases in the pens at the ranch. In my present work, I
need a jigger of castoreum every day."

There was a P. S.: "After I get my strength back,
I'm going to sell Beaverol to the natives. You can
handle production and I'll handle sales. You'll be
rich before you're forty."

Camellia Debut

Some plants have a hard time in the part of Fort Worth where I live. When their roots enter the limestone rock in my area these plants turn yellow, wither and die. I'm speaking of shrubs like camellias and trees like east Texas pines that require a lot of acid in their diet. Limestone, being alkaline, is murder for them.

I discovered plenty of limestone rocks beneath my yard when I dug a hole for a pine tree. My neighbor, Cobb, a sophisticated grower of camellias, said that pine trees would not grow in Fort Worth. But I've proved him wrong so far by giving my pine tree regular doses of acid during the growing season.

Cobb doesn't make many mistakes because he doesn't take many risks. From my backyard, I have a good view of the quonset arc of his greenhouse where he has over a hundred camellias growing in clay pots. I also have a good view of the pile of broken pots that he keeps building higher and higher. If I'm nearby when he pitches another broken one on the pile, he'll say that some people try to grow camellias in metal containers, but that's all wrong. Clay's the only thing.

Cobb makes growing camellias look easy. He

lets me watch him prune and fertilize his plants but never does   really explain certain things. Once I walked in on him when he was grafting a twig with two or three leaves on it onto the cut-off stalk of a plant. He said the twig was a camellia japonica scion that he was grafting onto camellia sassanqua root stock. He explained that sassanquas were easier to grow than japonicas.   Then, to impress me, he started talking about another type he called reticulatas. Confused, I asked him to explain, and he said I should join the Fort Worth Camellia Society if I was really interested, because growing camellias required more know-how than growing pine trees.

Cobb had know-how all right. The payoff for all of his skill and effort came during the blooming season, from November to March, when he would load up his van with blooms in styrofoam containers and head for a camellia show. I sometimes helped him load, feeling left out when he drove off. He travelled as far east as Shreveport and as far south as Houston. And he always came back home with a fistful of blue ribbons.

One Saturday last January, after watching Cobb leave very early for a show in Conroe, I came back in the house and stood at my window looking at the pine tree in my back yard. It was as green as any in east Texas, and I was proud of it. But I had a vague longing for more.

Later, as I was reading the morning paper, I saw an ad about a shipment of plants that one of the nurseries had just received. It occurred to me that if the nurseryman was willing to gamble on a whole truck load of camellias, why couldn't I plant just one?

A half-hour later, I was walking around in the nursery admiring the nurseryman's collection. When I asked him how to plant a camellia outside, he said to dig a hole twice as deep and twice as wide as the root ball and to plant it above any low spots where limestone water might percolate upward to the roots. Also plant it in the shade, out of the hot afternoon sun, but beware of the sun hitting the plant too early because of the danger of burning the leaves in winter before they have a chance to thaw. Don't over-water, but never let a plant dry out, he warned. Then he handed me a folder on how to fertilize. I could see that growing a camellia would be more complicated than caring for a more adaptable pine tree.

A little farther along my eyes fell upon a matching pair of white blossoms, and I stopped in my tracks. The tag said that the plant was a Nuccio's Gem, a camellia japonica with formal blossoms. Instantly, I had a vision: a plant, loaded with white blossoms, rose up beside my pine tree. Cobb sat in an upstairs window of his house with field glasses trained on my plant, which was so large it shielded his pile of broken pots. Still in a half-trance, I told the nurseryman I would buy it.

When I got home with my new plant I discovered that my wife had made plans for us, so I didn't get my camellia into the ground until after Cobb returned from Conroe. As I was digging the hole, he came out of his greenhouse with another broken pot, tossed it on the pile, and strolled over to watch me. In his confident way, he removed a handful of blue ribbons from his pocket and began whacking them against his pants leg, ignoring my struggles with a large limestone rock. I could feel his lukewarm grin as he stood over me, but I didn't look up.

After I got the rock out, I began lining the hole with a mix of sand, compost, and pine-bark mulch, as directed by the nurseryman. In a casual tone, Cobb said that I should have used one hundred percent peat moss instead. He added that everyone knows peat moss is best, and he whacked his ribbons again. I made no response, and he said an even better idea would be to leave my plant in the pot and put it in his greenhouse. Then I could plant another pine tree in the hole I had dug. Cobb said it was silly to plant a camellia japonica outside, especially one with white blossoms. If the freeze or the squirrels didn't get the blossoms, the trash falling from the trees above would ruin them.

I lowered my plant into the hole, then began packing soil mix around it. All the time, Cobb was shaking his head as if I was burying a loved one. When I finished, he said I should have bought a sassanqua and grafted a japonica scion onto it from one of his prize-winning plants. If I had joined the Camellia Society then I would know that's the way to win.

I had always suspected that Cobb kept things from me as a way of pressuring me to join the Camellia Society. As far as I could tell, the Society was just a mutual admiration group. Every year they had big shows and gave each other ribbons, silver cups, and bowls. Cobb had his awards on display in a cabinet in his dining room, and every time we went over there for dinner, I had to sit through the meal staring at them.

Cobb didn't mind visitors to his greenhouse. But sometimes, when I asked about a technical matter, like grafting, he would get sort of cagey. He showed me a thick book once, a nomenclature book he called it. If I wanted to know the characteristics of the hundreds of different plants--characteristics which a grower should know before grafting anything--then I would be well advised to buy one of these books. All the dope's in here, he said, leaving me to guess what he was talking about.

These visits to his greenhouse made me feel as if I'd bitten off more than I could chew. I began to wonder why I had not been satisfied with my pine tree. I'd ventured into the unknown, gambling on a plant that seemed to be as unpredictable as a young horse that had never won a race. Yet somehow it seemed like fun. I was betting on myself and my plant, both long shots.

In September, Cobb offered to take me to the first meeting of the year of the Fort Worth Camellia Society, and I decided I had better go. Cobb introduced me to some very nice people, not at all like him. As far as I could see, there wasn't a Paul Pry or a know-it-all in the bunch. During the program part of the meeting, a guest from Dallas explained fertilizing so that even I could understand. At one point, Cobb interrupted to say he had worked out a new wrinkle on gibbing, which he hoped to have time to tell about. The presiding officer said that would have to wait until the next meeting when gibbing would be the subject. Cobb sat down and everyone laughed.

I won a door prize, a bag of cotton seed meal, which I had just learned was the best fertilizer to use. Then everyone stood around and talked for a while, enjoying coffee, fruit juice, cookies and cake. The people were so friendly and the desserts so outstanding I decided to join.

At the October meeting, the program speaker brought one of his own plants for the gibbing demonstration. He showed me how to remove a growth bud next to a flower bud, and how to put a drop of gibberillic acid in the hole with a hypodermic needle. He said that the acid was a hormone that would stimulate the bud to produce a larger than normal blossom in about six weeks.

Subsequent meetings took up pruning, grafting, and plant diseases and insects. Cobb generously offered his opinion about each program speaker's recommendations. Others joined in, making the discussions lively and confusing. Each member seemed to have a slightly different slant on how to do everything.

The January meeting took up the annual show, to be held in mid-February at the Fort Worth Botanic Garden Center. Novices like me were urged to compete. A special table would be set aside for members who had never won a ribbon before.

The show chairman made it clear that all members were expected to pitch in to make the show a success, so I volunteered to help. We set up tables on Saturday morning, then everyone came back at seven on Sunday morning as the growers began arriving with their styrofoam boxes.

Cobb had commandeered a whole table for himself in a crowded corridor where he was busy filling out tags for his blooms and filling cups with water to put them in. All of his blooms looked gibbed, they were so big. When a shortage of medium-sized cups developed, Cobb complained loudly that someone had helped themselves to his hidden supply of that particular size. No one listened.

The blooms were placed on tables in alphabetical order and by size: extra large, large, medium, and miniature, with japonica blooms separated from the reticulatas. I found the novice table at the end of the display, and I set my flower down among blooms of every size and type. The competition for novices looked impressive. Although my flower was well formed, I hadn't gibbed it, so it wasn't all that big.

The judges worked in teams of three, with two clerks to handle the ribbons and staple the proper color onto the tag. I was teamed with a young lady who had worked before as a clerk. The judges took their work very seriously, bending over each table like doting grandparents over a cradle. Their ratings surprised me once in a while, and I began to hope that I might win a third-place ribbon, at least. But sometimes the judges marked a big "X" on a tag, and I knew that if that should happen to my flower, I would never get over it.

Finally the judges came to the novice table. They leaned over my entry for a long time, twisting their heads and squinting. Then they whispered. When one of the judges lifted my tag to mark it, I couldn't bear to look. After they passed on, my teammate picked up the tag and began waving it under my nose. She started laughing, and I felt sure my flower had been disgraced. But then I heard her saying that I had won a blue ribbon. I couldn't believe it! Still, there it was--a big check mark in the number one square.

All through the show that afternoon, I hovered near my flower in case any of my friends showed up in the line of spectators. None did. But at home the morning after the show, I made a plastic covering for my blue ribbon and went outside to hang it on my plant.

And just as I finished, Cobb came around the corner of his greenhouse with a pair of stem-cutters in his hand rather than the usual broken pot. He walked up to my plant, looked at the plastic tag, and without turning around, he said, "I suppose you don't mind if I clip a couple of scions, do you?"

DNA Made Simple

Late on a September afternoon, Dave and I are having a drink on my patio. Dave owns a ranch near the new Comanche Peak nuclear power plant at Glen Rose, sixty miles south of Fort Worth, and Dave is worried, as I am in this nuclear age, about survival of the human race in general and of ourselves in particular.

"Feel that breeze?" Dave asks, rattling the ice in his glass. "That wind just blew across the new plant. If that plant ever goes up, I can say good-bye to my ranch and you can say good-bye to your tomatoes."

"That's for sure," I say, getting up to refill his glass. While I'm inside, I dig out a newspaper clipping, and I bring it out to Dave.

"Talking about survival, did you read this article in the paper? It's about DNA. Ever hear of that?"

"A little." Dave's chair squeaks as he reaches and squeaks again as he settles back to read.

This article defines DNA as deoxyribonucleic acid, a genetic molecule that passes on the characteristics of the parent to succeeding generations. The theory is that the first cell on earth had one of these molecules to start the ball rolling, and that all living things have evolved from that first cell--plants as well as animals.

Dave finishes and looks up. "If I understand, they're saying all living things have a common ancestor, this DNA molecule."

"That's the way I understand it."

Dave folds the clipping and puts it on the table just as a gray lizard, almost a foot long and fat, scampers across the patio. I jerk involuntarily even though I see them all the time. This one catches a cricket before it can reach the lawn. They're called skinks. I like them, but I think of how awful it would be if one ran up my pants leg.

Standing up, Dave thanks me for the drink and invites me to go with him to his ranch the next day. He says that skink reminded him he has to pick up a horned lizard for TCU's biology department (Texas Christian University is just up the hill from my place). We can also stop at Dinosaur Valley State Park to see tracks left millions of years ago by giant lizards, if I would like.

While watering my tomatoes the next morning, I see teaspoons of earth being tossed into the air out of a shallow cut in the soft ground. Soon, I spy the tail and hind claws of the digger. The creature turns and takes a stand in the hole and begins to bob and weave and do push-ups at me. It looks like the fat skink we saw on the patio. Thinking the lizard is digging a hole to lay eggs in, I back away. I wouldn't want to disturb the nest of a future squadron of cricket-catchers.

A few minutes later, Dave honks and we set out. Between Granbury and Glen Rose, the tops of the silos of the nuclear power plant rise above the horizon. I lower my window as we get closer.

"The sight of those silos puts me on edge," I say.

Dave takes a quick look. "They bother me, too, but they're putting them up all over. Also Europe."

"There's no place for the waste," I say.

"Well, what would you do if you had the job of guaranteeing our energy supplies when we run out of fossil fuels?"

"The way things look, that will take a long time."

"It's my understanding that after we've burned enough coal, the greenhouse effect will be as bad as a nuclear explosion."

I close my window, wondering whether humans could survive such a development. Skinks and horned lizards would probably have a better chance.

South of Glen Rose we come to a sign saying Dinosaur Valley State Park, and Dave turns in.

"I want you to see this," he says. "Over a hundred million years ago, this area was a shoreline where dinosaurs lived. They say something happened suddenly and wiped them out."

Four miles farther on, we come to the entrance then drive to a parking area near the river.

"We'll get out here and walk," Dave says.

After picking our way across the limestone slabs of the river bed, Dave begins pointing.

"All these mixed-up tracks mean the dinosaurs had a big fight here. The meat eaters caught some vegetarians in shallow water."

I look at the tracks, having trouble grasping such a wide expanse of time. Am I to believe that during that epoch, as one species after another came and went, DNA kept twisting and turning and finally produced not only skinks and lizards but also humans?

I take a snapshot of Dave bending over one of the

tracks, then we get in the car and drive a short distance to an exhibit area where two life-sized replicas stand, a Tyrannosaurus and a Brontosaurus. As I read the sign, I wonder whether the evidence that humans leave behind will be as enduring as that left by the dinosaurs.

After leaving the park, we head south. Beyond Chalk Mountain the cedars retreat and the land flattens into semi-desert, broken by shallow arroyos. Dave says this is ideal horned lizard country. He turns onto a dusty ranch road that leads us through sparse pasture and bald limestone outcroppings until we top a rise and see a cluster of buildings gathered around a windmill, like hens flocked around a rooster. A boy jumps off the porch of the house and comes running up the road to meet us.

Dave gets out and sweeps the boy into his arms. "Good Lord, you're getting big!"

"I got your lizard, Grandpa!"

Dave looks inside the coffee can the boy is holding, then he eases the lizard into his hand, caressing the spines that run from the top of its head to the tip of it tail, like a midget Tyrannosaurus.

Turning to me, Dave says, "Here, hold him while I get his cage out of the trunk."

His stomach feels cool and smooth, like a skink's, I suppose, although I've never tried to catch a skink and never shall, for that matter. I am thinking this lizard is a hardy creature to survive in an area like this. What does he eat?

Dave brings the cage and sets it on the ground.

"Put him in here. Don't squeeze him, though. He might squirt blood on you."

I set the lizard carefully on the sand floor of the cage in the midst of swarming red ants. As the lizard settles into the sand, the ants within reach of his tongue begin to disappear. All of the ants have disappeared before Dave finishes telling his grandson good-bye.

Sitting on my patio, I listen to cheers from TCU's stadium up the hill and watch bombers rise from Carswell Air Force Base. Dave is probably in the stadium with his grandson rooting for TCU's horned frogs, a misnomer almost as old as Texas Christian itself. All the fans know TCU's mascot is a lizard and not a frog.

The bombers rise with a thrust of power greater than the dinosaurs. The giant lizards were programmed for power, just as these bombers are, but humans themselves aren't. We have options other than self-destruction, yet, like TCU football fans, we refuse to change, even though we know better.

If we continue to ignore the choices handed to us, we may have to face our collective destruction. But the earth and the molecule will continue, perhaps someday evolving creatures who may muse at our tracks and mount our bones.

Resorting
to
Simplicity

‿‿✦‿‿

Almost every place you go on vacation nowadays, you find remodeling, expansion, and new construction. Change is looked upon as the way to live. But at Coon's Lodge on Trout Lake, north of Woodruff, Wisconsin, change comes slowly and reluctantly, usually the result of some intrusive regulation. Growth isn't an article of faith at this resort, for Coon's is a place that tries to stay as it always has been. And this makes it the most exotic hideaway I know of.

You hear about Coon's through friends. On our first visit in August, 1962, we arrived at bedtime and met Mrs. Phil Coon at the desk in the lodge. She assigned us to Birchwood, one of the cabins on the two-mile stretch on the south shore of the lower lake. After talking about our mutual friends for a while, we started calling her Jimmy, which she prefers, although her real name is Mary.

The next morning, I awoke at dawn to the cry of a loon. I slipped out into the crisp, piney air in shirt sleeves then went back for a sweater. A mist hung over the lake, but I could make out an island through the branches of the trees. At the lake's edge, I stepped on a fallen branch, and immediately the startled call of a loon sprang up. Then a large bird splashed through the water and skimmed out of sight.

I followed the path along the lakefront until it reached a marina and beach area. The sun had driven off the mist and was shining on the tops of tall pines high above a flag pole in front of the lodge. A woman was doing laps to a pontoon anchored offshore, and a man in a windbreaker and cloth porkpie hat was tidying up the beach front. I stopped and watched him loop neat spirals of ropes on the hulls of sail boats lined up at the water's edge.

When he finished, he put out his hand.

"I'm Phil Coon," he said.

I introduced myself and said we had just arrived.

"Yes. You're in Birchwood. Ought to be big enough."

The woman got out of the water, and I saw it was Jimmy. She waved, then put on her beach robe and headed for their home above the marina boat house.

I asked Phil whether I could call him by his first name, and he said please do as he studied the limp flag on the pole. Then he observed, "Ought to be windy by afternoon. Good day for a sail."

"What's the temperature now?" I asked.

"Sixty-one," he said, and walked off toward the boat house carrying a load of life jackets and empty bottles.

One thing I learned early was that Phil Coon didn't burden his friends with a lot of unnecessary conversation.

I was in the Navy four years but never learned to sail until I got to Coon's. After lunch, I went down to the beach and Phil selected a boat for me. Not wasting a word, he told me about the rudder, the dagger board, and the sail rope then shoved me off with the comment it would be a good idea to stay in sight of the beach until I got some experience.

I did okay on the straightaways but kept capsizing on the turns. I know I must have gone over fifteen times. Finally, Phil came out in a motor boat and reminded me to ease up on the sail rope when I felt I was going over.

The next day I had no stomach for sailing: it was too sore. Instead, Phil Coon, Jr. (everyone called him Phillip) took us by motorboat to a picnic spot in the upper lake. There a wide strip of sand under a few inches of water made a playground for the young ones that was as much fun as the beach at the lodge.

Phillip came back in midafternoon to pick us up. He knew one speed, fast. We zoomed around the upper lake then headed south toward Coon's in the lower lake. Suddenly, Phillip said he would like to show us a muskie's nest. When we got close, Phillip cut the engine, and the boat drifted silently until we saw a large fish fanning an empty, gravelly bed. There were no small fry about, nor any fish eggs that I could see, but Phillip said it really was a nest.

Taking off again, with the boat's bow almost vertical, Phillip told us muskies are rare in Trout Lake because the clear water has little for them to eat. We churned a wide wake past Haunted Island-- the island I saw the first morning--and flew like the wind back to Coon's marina.

We've been going back to Coon's for almost twenty-five years, although in the meantime we moved to Texas from Wisconsin. While Texas summers are always hot, the temperature in northern Wisconsin isn't that predictable. Some years it rains often, and a temperature above seventy is rare. Other years the beach is crowded every day, but a jacket feels good at night.

Either way, everything there is always so green!

Coon's lures us back in another way too, for unlike some of our highly seasoned Texas cooking, meals at Coon's are unextravagant yet tasteful and nutritious. The kitchen has made only minor changes in the menu in all the time we've been going there. And since the selections repeat themselves every week, I never have to look at a calendar; if I've forgotten what day it is, I'll remember when the waitress announces the choices.

The living accommodations are like the food: natural yet edifying. At one time or another, we've stayed in the lodge itself as well as about half of the cabins--cabins with names like Fern Villa, Daybreak, Roughwood, Birchwood, Trail's End, Sleepy Knob, Dewdrop, and Beach. (No guest cabins have been added since the dining room was expanded many years ago, and the dining room seats only a few more than a hundred people.) We've stayed more often in Fern Villa and Roughwood than any of the others because Fern Villa is close to the lower tennis courts and Roughwood is close to the upper.

On rainy days, when tennis and sailing are on hold, I love to sit by the fireplace and read, like this morning when Haunted Island is barely visible through my window. After an hour or so of reading, I put on my boots and raingear and start out on the familiar trail by the lake. I should know every root and rock by now, but I trip. A loon's cry, far off, sounds a warning and I stand motionless. Then I hear a fainter answering call from Haunted Island. Today, their ululating duet seems to be mourning the loss of their friend, Phil Coon. Yesterday, I was telling Phillip (Phil, Jr.) how I accused his father of thinking as much of the loons as he did of the guests. Phillip said he wasn't sure about that, because he loved the virgin pines too.

The rain falls gently as I walk along the lakefront, past the boat house, past the flag pole and virgin pines, then past the sail boats lying there with their ropes neatly spiralled. I go into the lodge and step over the kids sprawled in front of the TV. After chatting for a while with Jimmy, I go out again. The lower tennis courts are empty. The smell of birchwood smoke hangs close to the ground, and I wonder what day it is. It's a peaceful day, nothing special, which is exactly why I'll be back next season.

Gutting Out

"Gutting Out" is the term my wife applies to cleaning out kitchen cabinets, refrigerators, freezers, storerooms, garages, and clothes closets. I try to be off the premises when she tears into one of these purges. For me, cleaning out a closet is a leisurely affair, a time for fondling old possessions and reliving moments of the past. Old things remind me of where I have been and how I have felt about situations. As part of the process, I do throw away a few things to please my wife, but in the end I always find that many things can't be eviscerated because my closet is really an extension of myself.

My closet is L-shaped, probably because of some error in the original house plans, but it suits me fine. The far end of the L is hidden, like the dark side of the moon. This is where I put things while trying to get up the nerve to throw them away. Deciding to toss some things out is like working up the courage to put an old dog to sleep.

The fumigators who came to our house one day propelled me into a purging mode. My wife had invited them but was away when they made their inspection. As they were leaving, the chief inspector said their spraying would be more effective if we could relieve congestion like that in the L-shaped closet.

I watched them go, realizing that the time for action had come. I would have to work fast, because we were going to the Armed Forces Day parade as soon as my wife returned.

Ignoring my current stuff in the front end of the closet, I tackled the far end. After several quick trips, I had spread out before me an assortment of shirts, pants, dressing robes, torn plastic raincoats, hats, caps, pajama bottoms, old uniforms, and T-shirts. I sailed first into the shirts and pajama bottoms.

If a shirt was torn or had a frayed collar, I tossed it on the floor, even though it had good buttons on it. I also pitched the pajama bottoms. These tended to accumulate for the reason that I always wore out the tops first. I knew my wife would be pleased if she could see how ruthless I had become.

Next came the T-shirts. It was easier to toss these since most of them were yellow anyway. Some had rips under the right arm from tennis, but none had any of those clever, spoofing labels that are so popular nowadays.

My caps were specimens of this labelling trend. One was white with scrambled eggs on the visor, and the other was bright orange with STUD printed on the crown. Both were gifts, and as my grandmother would have said, not fit to wear to the privy. Yet, I've seen fellows wearing similar ones in restaurants.

And here, in all their glory, were my two favorite hats: a gray Borsalino, and a cream-colored Midwestern type squashed flat with the torn edge of a railway Pullman ticket sticking out of the band. I pushed the crown out and tried it on, remembering that President Truman had worn a hat like this. It had given him that look of confidence and determination which was a reflection of his true self.

I could never part with such a gem. Besides, hats were on the way back, and would, I hoped, soon displace those silly caps.

I hung the Midwestern number back in the closet to await the day when men would once again wear hats with President Truman's resolute gestalt. Then I picked up the Borsalino. This was the type that President Roosevelt had been fond of wearing, tilted to one side or far back on his head to give clearance for his cigarette holder. President Roosevelt was the embodiment of self-confidence, and his Borsalino displayed his anima to the world. I put it on.

Looking into the mirror, I felt some of the electricity of the war years. Since President Roosevelt was a navy man, it was only fitting that I wear my Borsalino while checking through my uniforms.

Here was a suit of navy blues that I wore the day President Roosevelt visited our base during World War II. Since then, I've relied upon TV and the newspapers to learn what the president is like. Now that the trend to hats has returned, perhaps all of us will profit, because I think it's easier to know what a person is like if he's wearing a hat.

One of the last stacks on the bed was my pants. There were several pairs of peg legs: wide in the seat and knee, and narrow at the bottom. I took off my shoes to try on a pair. Although snug in the waist, this pair had pleats, making the seat even roomier. In one of the pockets, I found an aspirin tin with a three-cent stamp in it.

Pants styles, like hat styles, go in cycles, but you can never go out without your pants on. A public figure can throw his hat in the ring, but not his pants. Maybe that's why images are created by hats instead of pants.

Before I began gutting out, I had decided to throw away all of my old tennis shoes. They made a pile almost as high as the other rejectamenta. Getting rid of the shoes would improve the fragrance of my closet as well as its looks.

Now that I could see clearly inside my closet I spotted a collection of hard-cover books on the shelf. Standing on a stool, I took one down and recognized it as my mother's.

This book, a general history of mankind, covered all the ground from the time of ancient Egypt to 1906, the year it was printed. The original edition came out in 1895. My mother paid $1.41 to the State of Texas for it.

I recognized my mother's handwriting in a cryptic note on the fly page: "Always remember February 21, 1909." There was more writing on the other side in my father's hand that asked, "Do you love me?" My eye followed a line to the lower corner of the page where the answer "Yes" appeared. Below that were the words "I'm glad you do."

The back door slammed. I looked at the clock. Where had all the time gone!

When my wife entered the bedroom I greeted her in my peg-leg pants with the Borsalino tilted to one side of my head. I put my hands in my pockets and hopped around so she could get a good look.

"What on earth!" she said.

"I feel like going to a parade!" I said. "Come on, let's go!"

Listening to Myself and Others

∽◌ ◌∾

At the start of World War II, when I applied for commissioned officer status in the Navy (a maneuver intended to side-step the draft), I discovered that my hearing was not 4-0. After the Navy doctor's examination, I hurried home to our family G. P., who swabbed and sprayed all of the ducts, orifices and canals in my head and throat. The fogging and daubing worked beautifully. With the draft board breathing down my neck, I sailed at flank speed to another Navy recruiting station, where I heard the test watch ticking before the doctor took it out of his pocket.

After the War, I married a girl I'd met while in the service. She had a clear strong voice which carried well even when she whispered in church. And within a year or so, I realized her hearing was perfect, too. At night, while changing the baby's diaper, she could hear migrating birds flying above our house. And on certain spring evenings, she'd suddenly think she heard the neighbor's cat squashing her freshly planted petunias. But it wasn't until our children were through college that she began to complain that I wasn't listening as I should.

Since I'm a loner anyway and like reading more than socializing, I'd unconsciously begun to enjoy the greater privacy of the hard of hearing. Listening to the voices within had become more than a pastime with me. Of course, my experience wasn't as dramatic as that of the Biblical prophet Elijah who heard a single small voice, but I could privately tune in to the voices of old friends and the happy sounds of old times together. Unfortunately, during these lapses I missed a lot of what was going on around me, to my wife's growing irritation.

She would say, "The faucet's dripping. Don't you hear it?" Or she would want to know when I planned to change clothes for the party, and I would ask, "What party?" I often was accused of not paying attention to a word she said. Furthermore, she was convinced that I could hear anything I really wanted to hear.

In other situations, I noticed that I could no longer understand small children with their high, thin voices and rapid speech, while our poodle, with her wider range of hearing, seemed to have no trouble at all. (It occurred to me that grown-ups with high voices may be surprised to find out how much of what they say is heard only by dogs.)

While watching TV, I couldn't understand people like Barbara Walters who mumble, nor others with strong accents, like Katharine Hepburn. Anyone with an accent, no matter what kind, might as well have been speaking Etruscan.

Under these deteriorating circumstances, I consciously made an effort to listen. This was hard work, something I'd never had to do before. In the past, I had always been able to pick up a word here and a phrase there to follow the gist of the conversation. But now I had to cup my ear and try to read the speaker's lips.

The results were not always satisfactory. Some people, seeing me cup my ear, would raise their voices for a sentence or two then resume their normal manner of speaking. I knew sometimes they were annoyed, and I certainly didn't like being spoken to in a loud voice, either.

My wife, however, made no move to change her speaking habits. She continued to address me through bathroom doors or from around the corner of the house. Once, I asked her to please face me while speaking so I could receive the full impact of the sound waves. It was the futility of that request that drove me to seek a hearing aid.

The first hearing aid I bought plugged into our TV. It had a cord about twelve feet long, which meant the user could sit across the room from the TV screen and trip unwary guests. An ear plug was attached to the other end of the cord, but I don't care to meet the human being whose ear was used as a pattern for the plug. Instead of having a normal, curved aural canal, this person must have had a hole in his head made by an arrow.

The next device I experimented with was at church in the pew reserved for the hearing impaired. Since this pew was usually unoccupied, I supposed that not many of the hard of hearing attended church--or that if they did, they sat in regular pews and felt no great loss from missing most of what was said.

One Sunday, my wife suggested that we sit in the reserved pew, perhaps figuring I needed the sermon as much as she did. After we were seated, I saw before me a plastic cup and an amplifier box connected by a tension cord. When the sermon began, I jockeyed the cup into position over my ear and turned up the volume. The plastic cup fit about as well as an empty tomato can and was about as effective. As I sat there trying to improve the reception, I began to understand why the reserved pew was usually empty.

It was not as though I suffered from a severe handicap (although I did have a new awareness of wheel-chair victims who have no way of getting from their chairs onto those special restroom seats reserved for them). I could hear as well as, for example, a worm. Relatively speaking, worms hear quite well. When they hear the guillotine of my spade approaching, worms come squirting out of the ground in my garden like toothpaste from a tube. While I could hear as well as a worm, I wasn't much better off. My environment of racing fire trucks and impatient motorists posed as great a threat to me as any spade to any worm.

During the time that I was visiting various hearing aid places, I happened to break my glasses, frames and all. After many visits and many   discussions-- and still plagued with doubt--I bought a pair of glasses with an antenna in one temple and an amplifier in the other, the two being connected by a wire across the nose piece. A tube extended downward from one temple into my ear, and the other temple housed a small battery for amplifying sound waves.

The audiologist fitted the tube into my better ear and warned me that increasing the audibility of this ear would decrease my stereophonic capability. He also said that sudden, harsh sounds might cause some discomfort, and that background noise would be a problem. He was right on all counts.

On my way home from his office, a young man in a high-powered racing vehicle took off next to me at a red light and almost split my ear drum. Later the shriek of our garage-door apparatus taught me the importance of adjusting the volume in advance.

While some new devices are supposed to make automatic volume adjustments, the stereophonic problem, when it gets bad enough, is usually corrected with an aid in each ear. Not wanting to go that far, I disconnected our back doorbell when I found I couldn't determine whether the front or back bell was ringing. But coping with background noises and large crowds was something else.

I've never been to a cocktail party where a premium was put on listening, and this particular party was no exception. When the crowd really got going, I had to disconnect my battery--the clamorous babble sounded like the squawking of a hundred kazoos.

It was worse than having no aid at all. A normal ear will dampen sounds it doesn't want to hear, such as background music and chatter at a noisy party. A hearing aid makes no such discrimination (or very little, in the same manner that eye glasses do not correct color-blindness). Whatever hits a hearing aid antenna gets amplified, in my case especially the higher notes (shorter sound waves), because these are the frequencies my hearing aid was designed to amplify most.

Eventually, I had to get rid of my glasses, not because of the hearing aid installed in them, which was just as good as any other, but because they were too heavy. My nose is thin at the point where the glasses rest. To be comfortable, I needed a

Roman nose with skin as tough as cowhide.

My new hearing aid fits wholly within my ear and is as advanced as any on the market, although I've seen some without batteries. Mine is supposed to filter and dampen unwanted sounds, but I remove it at loud parties. Just like my first one, it clears up tinnitus, and it also gives the sound of my own voice a strange, tambourine quality. Voices in the upper ranges still sound like Rudy Vallee singing through a tin megaphone. And I can't pick up Katharine Hepburn word for word on TV without closed captions.

Although continuous improvements are being made in the conduction of sound waves, I'm not aware of similar advances being made in their reception, especially in that mysterious inner ear where the conversion of sound waves into electrical impulses takes place. Until that's done, the installation of more woofers and tweeters won't do me any good. I have to depend on my imagination to cope with sound blindness. And locked deep in my mind are some vivid sound tracks from the past.

We live on a street which dead ends at a pond, one of my favorite places for taking excursions into the past. In summer, the pond is populated with bull frogs and other creatures that chirp, twitter, trill and splash. It gets so noisy at times that we call it the Pond of Babel.

One night not long ago as I stood beside the pond listening to the cacophony, a mosquito lit on my hearing aid with the whining shriek of a dive-bomber. I quickly disconnected my battery to shut off the amplifier. Then everything got so still that I could have been in outer space. I felt, rather than heard, the deep bass of the bull frogs, throbbing in unison with the chords of the universe. My own heart-beat seemed to pick up the cadence, and I waited, listening.

Soon, from across the pond, voices of the past floated to me. I distinctly heard a joyous Thanksgiving--the laughter of women in the kitchen and the drone of men's voices around the fireplace. The scene changed, and a deafening roar went up in a crowded gymnasium. A boy shouted in my ear, "Daddy, Daddy! We won!" As the roar subsided, the moon rose, and I sat on a porch watching lightning bugs twinkle and listening to a train whistle a mile away.

Then I was at a Scottish Bobbie Burns festival, and I saw the knobbed knees of a kilted giant pumping high as he led a bagpipe band and waved a seven-foot baton. The hair on the back of my neck rose at the sound.

You may think that sounds like these don't exist, that all sounds continue outward into space and eventually fade away, but they do not. They don't go very far at all. They stay right here. Locked in here, between my heart and my brain.

Tennis Forever

I've played tennis since I was a kid. While others have played longer and with greater skill, my game is my own, like my feet, my weak arches, and my arthritic shoulder. Tennis is part of my life and I love it.

Driven by a yearning for fame, I got off to a fast start in the small high school I attended. I learned to serve well, to anticipate my opponent's next shot, and to watch the ball so closely that, like Rod Laver, I could sometimes see the seams revolve.

Fame in those days meant doing well before a small crowd of mothers, sweethearts, coaches, teammates, and younger players who were forced to attend. The first time I competed at a county meet, the crowd of strangers was so large I tightened up and lost.

But after I won the county singles in my senior year, I thought I was pretty good. My self-esteem was soaring, blinding me to the level of competition I would face at the University.

At the first session, the freshman coach tried to scare off as many as he could. The fundamental rule was to win, he said. If something hurts, play anyway but play good. The best way to go, he advised, was to drop dead on the court in the heat of battle. He gave us a mean look, and no one asked any questions.

The first player I met was a six-foot, six-inch left-hander who took ground strokes with either hand. Spread out, he could reach halfway from one sideline to the other. He apologized for beating me. If he had only left it there, I wouldn't have felt so crushed, but he went on to say that he had eased up in the second set.

I was still demoralized from that match when I met Frankie at intramurals. Frankie was from a small town and had suffered the same kind of comeuppance as I, only it hadn't dampened his spirits. He darted around the court like an armadillo--a shell-encased animal faster than a runaway pig--and rushed the net at every opportunity. From the very first meeting, we were friends.

We played often and without restraint, smashing, squatting, dancing while the sweat washed down our backs. Sometimes when Frankie and I were playing, I would reach the point that every player wants with all his heart--the point when I seemed to be watching myself play. Suddenly, I knew where Frankie would place his next shot before my return crossed the net.

Following graduation, Frankie and I separated. Without Frankie for regular, inspired play, my game slowed down but my arthritis did not.

As the years passed, my game went farther downhill. On really bad days, I played a game called Triples where there are three players on each side of the net. Playing this game with fellows who had steel rods where their hip bones used to be made me ashamed to mention the ache in my shoulder.

In summer, Frankie and I usually got together for some geriatric tennis, as he called it. Once at a resort which catered to players of our caliber, I sat down on a bench to tighten my shoe laces, unaware that hornets had built a nest on the underside. I didn't intend to rile them up, but at least a dozen swarmed over me, stinging my back, my legs, and my shoulder. I danced around, flailing away with my racket. The players on nearby courts stopped to watch as Frankie was doing. Then he began swatting, too, but he laughed so hard he wasn't much help.

The next day, my shoulder felt better than it had in a long time and I beat Frankie easily. He said I was playing as if I had been reborn.

The rebirth didn't last long. After I got home, the old feelings returned and I slipped back to my former level of play.

The next summer we returned to the same place. When the sun settled near the horizon, after most players had quit for the day, Frankie and I set out for the courts. This evening, as I was checking nearby benches for hornets, a little kid came out of the pro shop and ran up to the fence.

"Hello, there," I said. "Want to hit a few?"

No answer, but his lips worked as he stared.

The pro shop door opened again and a young woman hurried out. She ran to the fence, took the little boy's hand, and began leading him away.

"We've got to get home. It's time for supper. Daddy will be waiting."

"Why? Those old men don't have to."

Frankie won serve and we began. As the pop of our rackets ticked off the last minutes of daylight, I

wondered how that little kid knew Frankie and I
would rather play than eat.

Reunion in Hughes Springs

How can you pick up where you left off with people you haven't seen for fifty years? A few, like Leita and Pepper, I had seen from time to time, but as for many of the others--it would be easier meeting total strangers. With outsiders, you wouldn't feel as though you had to reunite.

After three hours of driving, I took a coffee break in Mount Pleasant and told the waitress I was headed for my fiftieth reunion. As she was refilling my cup, I asked her whether she had ever worked at the cafe's old location on Highway 67 west of the courthouse. She said she had not and, for my information, fifty years was longer than she had been on this earth.

I left Mount Pleasant on State Highway 49, reminding myself to watch for the spot a few miles south where the prairie plays out and the pine trees begin. Soon I saw it, and I lowered my window to let West Texas air out and East Texas air in.

East of Daingerfield, the dirt got redder, the pine trees taller, and the hills steeper. Just beyond Gun Hill, I passed over the railroad track at Deep Cut, and then I entered the pretty little valley known as Hughes Springs.

When I reached the center of town, I saw a banner strung across Main Street, but it was not for our class. Instead, it proclaimed the merits of the football team and must have cost several times as much as the cost of publishing our school paper, the "Glancer". Along Main Street, I didn't see a single business that had taken out ads, except for the bank, and McMillan's Auto. A new Dairy Queen stood near the spot where Uncle Hilly had published the "New Era" and set type free for the "Glancer".

As I approached the First United Methodist Church, I saw cars and pickups clustered there like filings around a magnet. I parked across the street on the site of the northern church, remembering how its few remaining members had hauled down their flag and joined us southerners to put us temporarily ahead of the Baptists.

I heard the choir bearing down as I climbed the steps of the church where I had won a certificate for not missing a Sunday. Now Uncle Russell, in a blue suit and looking young, ushered me to a pew in front of the pulpit behind which stood two robed ministers and, above them, the choir. I recognized the older minister, Brother Gardener, who winked at me as if to forgive my late arrival. As I edged into the pew, the well-fed, gray-headed people sitting there gave me the impression, just for an instant, that I was looking at friends of my parents.

The choir finished with a seven-point Amen, and the young minister stepped down in front of the pulpit and asked the young children to come forward. Sitting in a circle on the floor, the small ones looked up at him while he explained the scripture, just as Aunt Ida had done Sunday after not-miss-a Sunday.

When Brother Gardener rose to speak, I wondered what he had talked about in his baccalaureate sermon fifty years ago. If he repeated it, word for word, would anyone know?

He began by saying how nice it was to be invited back to preach to a congregation still close to his heart, especially since the people in the front pews reminded him so much of their parents. He announced that after the service, all of the 1933 high-school graduating class would go down to the Spring Park for a box lunch, but that he would have to say good-bye at the church because of the long drive ahead. He had driven in early on Saturday from Houston so that he could visit in the stores on Main Street. But all of the stores were closed, even McMillan Auto, and there were only a few pedestrians. No one walked any more. (I glanced at Cousin Nevelle McMillan, thinking how unchanging he was but how the vehicles he sold had wrought so many changes.) Brother Gardener then said he had visited the Spring Park and found it just as it had been, a place of quiet beauty where he had gone so often to compose his thoughts.

As Brother Gardener got into the meat of his sermon, I glanced as far to the right as I could without turning my head. Half of those I could see wore glasses, and I saw one hearing aid besides my own. Other devices, such as suspensories, arch supports, incontinent pads, prostate implants, pacemakers, and artificial breasts, were hidden. If Uncle Balda were alive, he would recommend water from the Spring Park for all these disabilities. When my brother, Johnnie, and I had played in the Park, he had come daily to fill his water jug.

"You boys drinking plenty of this water?"

"Yes, sir," Johnnie answers.

"Be sure and drink plenty. Puts iron in your bones till they're like magnets. When you're magnetized, it's like being immunized, energized, and vulcanized."

The organ began playing, and I realized that Brother Gardener had stopped speaking. He and the young minister were standing before the pulpit inviting those not yet baptized to step forward. (Uncle Balda always said a person should be magnetized on spring water before he was baptized.)

After prolonged hugging and handshaking following the service, some of us walked down the slope to the Park. The Baptists hadn't arrived because their preachers never knew when to quit. While waiting, we gathered around L. J., our math and Spanish teacher, who had also coached football, basketball, tennis, and track. I asked him about the sports program in Hughes Springs.

"They've won some championships, and they should. They've got eight people coaching and not a one of them has to do any teaching."

Paul spoke up, "It's a much larger school now."

"Not eight times," L. J. said.

"Do they publish a high-school paper now?" I asked.

No one seemed to know.

Five cars pulled up at the north entrance and someone said the Baptists were finally coming. We all went to greet them with as much enthusiasm as if they had been Methodists.

Roy, one of the Baptists, said he had come all the way from Jackson, Mississippi. His father, who had been the Baptist minister in the early thirties, had a large family and had had to do carpentry work to supplement his minister's pay. While we talked, Roy looked up at the ceiling of the spring house.

"My dad and I put a new ceiling up there in 1932."

"You did a good job, if that's the same one."

"It is. I recognize the hammer-head marks. I did most of the job while my dad and Brother Gardener sat in a corner and talked about their congregations."

Meanwhile, loyal, dependable Ruth, who had organized the whole affair, was passing around box lunches. When all were served, I joined Leita, former cheerleader and guiding force of the class of '33, to look at copies of the "Glancer", and other memorabilia various members had brought.

"I just re-read your editorial," Leita said. "Do you remember it?"

How could I ever forget it? She was teasing, but I loved her for asking. I wrote and re-wrote my editorial for a week, then put it on the front page because I thought it was seminal stuff. I glanced at it, the familiar words coming instantly into my memory.

"It sounds a little sophomoric now," I said. "But I like the tone."

"Are you still that optimistic?"

"It's hard to say. There have been so many changes."

"We haven't changed. We're all still the same as we were long ago, but all that's happened to us in fifty years covers up what's inside, like layers of lava rock."

Of course, Leita is right. I'm glad I went to my

fiftieth reunion. It lasted long enough to say hello to everyone but not long enough to find out how different our lives have been. Revealing our experiences would make us feel like strangers. And the important thing is to preserve those images of one another as we were fifty years ago.

The Underground Enemy

Since moving to Texas from Wisconsin, I've gone to war every summer against swarms of creepers, crawlers, and jumpers from the insect world. The insects come at me from cracks in the earth that must reach down into a vast underground insect kingdom where billions of eggs hatch into larvae during the cooler months. As spring gives way to summer, rainfall stops, the soil splits, and the larvae begin to move. In July, the sun gets hotter and hotter and the fissures grow wider and wider even though I pour enormous quantities of water on my lawn and flower beds. The doves in the cedar elms, praying in their special language, repeat over and over, "Oh, Lord, please send rain," as a final apocalyptic warning. I never had this problem in Wisconsin. As I spray enemy tunnels that branch out in every direction, I understand why Texas covets Wisconsin water.

The doves, sparrows, bee martins, woodpeckers, frogs, and lizards would be a great help if they could be trained to destroy eggs and larvae. But they seem content to feast only on adults, and of these, they consume only as many as they need to satisfy their hunger.

Soon after we moved in, my adversaries from the bug underworld launched their first strike from the cedar elms towering over the west side of our house. Like the Japanese at Pearl Harbor, they achieved total surprise. Before I realized what was going on, I was surrounded by crawling waves of inchworms that had sneaked from the trees down the chimney in the dark of night, then marched across floors and up walls, covering furniture and drapes with spidery camouflage. The clusters were so thick that they screened out the early morning sun. And they came down faster than I could sweep them up.

I had to fight all alone, for my wife retreated to the hallway after crushing an enemy bunker between her toes. As she stood on one foot hollering, I tried to think of new tactics to stem the larval blitz. What general would have ever thought of using troops too young to shave on such a scale as this? These larvae couldn't fly away, so they had to win or die.

Finally, I hit on building a fire with newspapers in the fireplace. This worked. When the smoke began rising up the chimney, the youthful enemy fell onto the fire in such great numbers that they almost smothered it.

I claimed a victory of sorts, then gathered up several gallons of live and barbecued inchworms in a bucket. As I did this, I took a good look at one of these squishy wigglers that was not yet dry behind the ears. I noted he did not even have feet in his midsection. Being thus limited, an inchworm drew himself up into a loop, then extended his front end forward until he flattened, finally pulling up his rear to make a new loop.

While cleaning up the mess on the floor, I thought

about recruiting more allies. My present helpers--birds, frogs, and lizards--weren't aggressive enough. Too many adults survived and laid the groundwork for the next generation. Other species that relished larvae, like moles and shrews, were a possibility, but I decided they may create more problems than they would solve. Insecticides seemed to be the only answer, so I bought a two-gallon pressurized sprayer and a litre of bug killer.

One morning while on reconnaissance with my sprayer, I saw some wasps congregating high up under the eaves near the chimney. In this area, chimneys seem to appeal to insects as places for bivouac. If I ever build another house in Texas, I think I'll delete the fireplace and put the money into a greenhouse. My plants and I would be safer there--like villagers inside a walled fortress--and I wouldn't have to worry about allies.

Looking upward, I saw the wasps entering small cracks between the molding and the bricks while other wasps continued arriving to join the swarm. Darting and circling, they waited their turn to get through the opening into the attic. My sprayer wouldn't reach such a height, so I decided to check the loft from the inside.

When I got to the top of the attic access ladder, I saw thousands of wasps clinging to the rafters while others milled around looking for a place to land. I balanced myself on the ceiling joists like an airplane spotter and thought of another time when my ship sat beached at Okinawa as enemy air craft wheeled and turned in the distance preparing for their last run.

The wasps must have seen me and sounded the alarm, because a small formation broke away from the main swarm and headed toward me like kamikazes. As they made their dive, I ducked as low as I could and strained to reach a strap holding up an air conditioning duct. I didn't make it. Instead I swayed, lost my balance, and stepped through the gypsum board ceiling of the living room.

One leg went all the way through and my foot dangled just above the piano, while the other leg and one of my elbows caught on a joist. I was hurting so, hanging there like a broken crucifix, that I didn't notice the wasp stings.

After examining me, the doctor said I had some torn cartilage in my knee and that it would take a long time to heal even if I stayed off it. He also said he didn't want to frighten me, but I was lucky not to be sensitive to wasp stings. Some people react violently, he said, going into comas, even dying in some cases. He advised daubing my wheals with vinegar and taking it easy with a pillow under my knee.

That was two days ago. While partially immobilized, I've been enlarging my stockpile of weapons. At the hardware store, the salesman showed me a can of wasp killer that he called "star wars". It shoots a searing stream of instant death twenty feet into the air. I also bought a couple of bags of insecticide granules--the salesman called them "land mines"--but with the health of my allies in mind, I haven't spread them on the lawn yet.

The hot summer wears on parching grass, searing leaves, and widening the cracks in the soil for the convenience of egg-laying adult bugs. Frogs hide under rocks, lizards doze on hot brick walls, and doves pray for a miracle of rain. Knowing that rain isn't likely until after Halloween, I'm working on a plan. I intend to decorate the cedar elms with Chinese lanterns containing gypsum squares impregnated with cyanide. Any bug inhaling the vapor from one of these lanterns will be a terminal case and can be disposed of without danger to birds, frogs, and lizards.

If my idea works, it could be used safely without that awful zapping noise the electric bug killers make. And instead of trying to drown the underground enemy, more Texans could use the Chinese lantern method. If enough Texans did this, the egg-laying bug population would be reduced to less threatening size. Then the clamor over water would die down, friendly relations with Wisconsinites would be re-established, and peace would reign once more.

Epilogue:
The Last Gasp

I had put off writing about weeds until the month of February, because it's then that winter weeds in Fort Worth sneak out of the ground and lie hidden under the dead lawn grass--waiting to pop up in March like Jacks-in-the-Box spraying seed all around. But now the piece didn't seem to want to be written. I felt I needed a change of scene.

The cursor on the blank face of my computer blinked annoyingly as my fingers lay idle on the keyboard. My old typewriter was less obtrusive: it just sat there like a lump of coal until I punched it. Instead of concentrating on weeds, my mind lingered over a travel ad I'd seen of an island in the Caribbean where almost everyone spoke English and they said you could drink the water.

I got up and called a travel agent who said yes, the ad was true, but there were few shops, no tennis courts, no golf courses, and the cruise ships passed it by. It was a place for swimming, diving, and snorkeling, but little else besides lying on the beach. It sounded perfect.

I went into the kitchen to make more coffee, then I came back, passed by my computer, and stopped to stare at my bookcase.

Half of the shelves were cluttered with memorabilia of my life before I started trying to write. With my mind on warm breezes and white sand, I began polishing the pig figurines I'd accumulated in Milwaukee during my years in the meat-packing business. After finishing the pigs, I picked up a photo I took of our family in Salt Lake City with Mount Olympus in the background; I set it back among three pairs of discarded eyeglasses, an assortment of paperweights, a bottle of solidified paper cement, and a jar of dried chili pepper seeds. I was thinking how hard it is to write day after day, especially about weeds I hated anyway. In business, most tasks repeat themselves day after day; whereas in writing, each paragraph is new.

The phone rang. The travel agent said he'd found a vacancy in a guest house at the windward end of the island. There wasn't much of a beach, but it was the best place for diving. I took it, although I only snorkelled, and my wife didn't swim at all. The change of scene would do us both a lot of good, I thought

The island was a mirage of summery dreams after February in Fort Worth. The guest house sat on the edge of a coral cliff above a cove and a half-moon beach. The food was good although the rooms were small. Looking out of our window was like looking out of a porthole. I loved it, but my wife commented upon the lack of shopping in the village.

The younger couples in the guest house spent all day diving and most of the night on the deck which jutted out from the dining room. When my wife wasn't wandering around the village, she sat on the deck reading and glancing down at me on the beach below. She didn't like to go down the slippery stairs to the boat pier and beach.

Each morning, the motor boat left the pier with a load of divers and took them to a pontoon anchored above a sunken ship outside the cove. I watched the divers slide like black seals into the water. The boatman, wearing a vermilion life jacket rather than a black diving suit, didn't return to the pier. He stayed on the pontoon to wait for the divers.

I never ventured outside the cove. Instead, I swam to a buoy anchored to a submerged tugboat engine about a hundred yards from the beach. One of the waiters said I could climb down the buoy anchor cable if I wanted to see large fish weaving in and out of the cylinders.

But I couldn't hold my breath long enough to go down the cable, and my swimming wasn't that good. I swam better on my back because of an injury to my left leg in a fall during hand-to-hand combat with wasps. Also, the beach gradient was so steep I had trouble getting a foothold in the loose sand. Worst of all, a cramp in my good leg from over-exertion would be disastrous.

I usually had the beach to myself, except for the gulls and sand crabs. Lying there soaking up the sun, I felt my muscles letting go, and I tried not to think of writing. I was so relaxed I didn't think of sunburn either until my skin turned as red as the boatman's jacket.

Next morning, after the divers took off in the motorboat, I went down the stairs to the beach, taking along plenty of skin oil. I was reading in the shade of the cliff when I saw this sand crab standing beside his hole. His black eyes stuck out on stalks, rotating like police car lights, and he trembled all over like a racehorse at the starting post. He took a few steps to his right, then tacked to the left. In a quick reverse, he pounced on something that I couldn't see. He boxed with it for a while then ate it and went back into his hole. He must have been that white because he stayed in the sun only long enough for a quick lunch.

That night, when I told my wife about the sand crab, she said that was another reason she didn't go down to the beach. I knew she wasn't having as good a time as I was. She preferred a more turbulent environment, cluttered with people and talk. She seemed happier jostling with crowds and chatting with sales ladies in duty-free shops. I decided it was time to leave, but I wanted one more swim to the buoy.

At breakfast, I commented to the waiter about the choppiness of the water and asked whether the divers would be going out. He said that much chop wasn't bad at all and that they go out when it's much dustier than today.

I waited until the diving boat left, then I made my way down the steps to the beach and headed for the buoy. Swimming backstroke, I could see my wife standing on the deck scanning the horizon with binoculars like a woman waiting for her husband's ship to come in. She had said, regardless of the waiter's opinion, she didn't like the looks of the clouds. The deeper waves this morning slowed me down, and the snorkelling gear around my neck was no help. I had no flippers, but I got some use of my weak left leg as long as I swam on my back.

After reaching the buoy, I looked at the pontoon. The boatman was standing with his feet spread wide to keep his balance. As I watched, the divers began surfacing all around the pontoon. Then a misty shroud obscured my view.

The wind shifted. Thinking a waterspout was entering the cove, I began stroking for shore.

I didn't get very far swimming on my back because the waves kept washing over my mouth and nose. I rolled over, swimming sidestroke, kicking as hard as I could with my good right leg.

When I got closer to the beach, I saw my wife running up and down like a mother hen, and lugging a life preserver almost as big as she was. About that time, I gasped for air at the wrong moment and inhaled sea water instead. Nausea set in, and my good leg locked into a cramp. Although still afloat, I realized I might not make it.

I saw my wife fling the life preserver. Against the wind, it didn't go far. If I ever got that close, I'd be safe, but out where I was, I could barely touch bottom with my weak leg. And when a wave came along and lifted me into shallower water, I didn't have enough strength in that leg to withstand the pull of the undertow.

It was beginning to look as if my writing career would never see the light of day (up to this point it had been a well-kept secret anyway). I hadn't thought of dying this soon. If I had, I would have tried writing something significant about the meat-packing industry, the gas pipeline industry, the accounting profession, or perhaps an insightful piece on the economic situation in general. I didn't even have a eulogy for myself. Here I was on my way to a watery grave, and all I had to show were little things about cats, tennis, hearing aids, insects, over-crowded closets, and women in business. I felt caught off-guard and overwhelmed. I quit trying to keep my mouth above water. Soon, my bum leg played out altogether and I succumbed to an overall sense of relief.

When I came to, I was lying in the sand and someone was holding my head. My mouth tasted awful. I tried to raise up, but a soft hand held me down.

After we got home, my wife selected a wrist-watch for the boatman, and I wrote him a letter. But writing any more than that was hard. I was still shaken by my close call, and the heavy thunderstorms romping across north Texas during March kept me in a nervous state. This afternoon, a funnel cloud touched down on a nearby lake, and tonight, a man was interviewed on TV who had been on the shore of the lake at the time. He said he was running for shelter when he saw two fish land on the ground directly in his path. Then he looked up and saw a whole school of fish whirling in the air above his head, along with about a half-dozen frogs.

This morning, as I sit at my computer staring at the blinking light, I marvel at the fact of fish and frogs flying through the air. It's almost enough to change my thinking about leaving home to find a fresh approach. Going to a Carribbean island is fun, although sometimes risky, but for writers, greater wonders may be lying as close as a nearby lake--and perhaps closer than that. A new idea may be hiding in the tall weeds which sprang up while we were gone. I should be out there pulling them up. Who knows? I may discover a creature more exotic than a sand crab.